OUT OF GREAT
TRIBULATION

OUT OF GREAT TRIBULATION

by

HUMBERT WOLFE

LONDON
VICTOR GOLLANCZ LTD
1939

PRINTED IN GREAT BRITAIN BY RICHARD CLAY AND COMPANY, LTD. (T.U.),
BUNGAY, SUFFOLK.

Many of these poems have been published over a period of years. Grateful acknowledgment is made to the Journals in which they have appeared.

Special permission was obtained to republish the group of poems in the section entitled " Winter ", which had previously appeared in an anthology published by Messrs. Eyre & Spottiswoode, for me, under the title of *The Winter Miscellany*.

DEDICATION

LAUREL

IT was night when I came home
        bringing my sheaves,
an armful of bracken, and some
        fugitive leaves.

This is all that I had found
        at my soul's peril,
this rusty fern, these browned
        leaves for my laurel.

Let my lovers and haters
        tear them apart,
trampling like satyrs
        over my heart.

Let them tear them, or weave them
        about my brow.
They are theirs.   I leave them
        for ever now.

CONTENTS

Page

DEDICATION: Laurel   7

OUT OF GREAT TRIBULATION

Out of Great Tribulation   17
A Chant   18
The Negro Slave   19

AT THE END OF THE AVENUE

The Child Unborn   23
The Spearman   24
The Cypriot   25
Into the Dark   26
Purcell, Lawes or Lully   27
Down-Leaning to Thine Urn   28
The Calm Mountain-Valleys   30
The Painted Flower   32
At the End of the Avenue   33
An Armful of Bracken   34
Let Me Be Glad of Pain   35
The Fallen House   36
How Shall We Overtake   37
The Light-Footed   38
When You Look Back   39
Before the Stars Pass   40
The Snow-dictated Peace   41

AT THE END OF THE AVENUE (*continued*)

Peter's Plough 42
Two Obols 43
The Cold Unspoken and Angry Years 44

HAIL AND FAREWELL

Song and Sight 47
The Eastern Well 50
Liebestod 51
A Prayer 52
The Stone God 53
The Wood Nymph Speaks 54
The Corinthian Garlands 55
Extreme Diamond 56
The Gardenia 57
A Vow 58
He Asks a Promise 59
Exodus 60
You Must Not Ask 61
The Deserted God 63
Dispossession 64
The Flower 65
Red Shoes 66
The Blue Goddess 67
Nightingale-Throated 68
Return 69
All But Fallen City 70
The Rib of Adam 71
I'll Not Be Silent 72
I Praise Other Women 73
Death Will Not Guess 74

QUESTIONS AND NO ANSWERS

Light Balances 77
Milton Agonistes 78

QUESTIONS AND NO ANSWERS (*continued*)

My Thought	79
Monk of the Heart	80
The Yellow Rose	81
Victoria, the Lost Leave-Trains	82
The Bellringers	83
Dimensional	85
This Is Not Death	86
Purgation	87
Gently as the Grass Grows	88
The Launch	89
Spring	90
Inviolate Stranger	91
Let Not Your Heart	92
Troy	93
Parts of Speech	95
Pierrot Again	96
The Mask	97
For the Twenty-fifth Year	98
Coronation	99

PLACES

A Song of Compasses	103
Bradford	104
Labor Omnia Vincit—I	106
Labor Omnia Vincit—II	106
Labor Omnia Vincit—III	107
The School	108
Sport at Minehead	110
Hollings Hill	112
Aberuchill	113
Venice	114

Page

PLACES (*continued*)

Ashford Chace   115
Iceland   116
Another Way   117
Green Lemons   119
Fitzroy Street   120
The Fir Tree and the Palm   121

CONVERSATIONS

Conversation Galante   125
How a Girl Saw It   127
How a Man Saw It   130
The Game   132
God and the Devil   134
Jesus and His Friend   135
King and Cat   137
Pavane   138
The Card-Party   139
The Characters Upbraid the Author   142
The Answer   144

THE PIER-GLASS

The Pier-Glass   147
The Apple Trees   149
Hares   150
Music in Silence   151

EIGHT SONNETS

Dedication   155
Don Quixote   156
Lambs   157
This Night   158
Ursuline   159

12

Page

EIGHT SONNETS (*continued*)

    Quiet   160
    Unplucked, a Mountain-Lily   161
    The Last Sonnet   162

WINTER

    Winter   165
    Countryman's Winter   167
    Traveller's Winter   168
    Soldier's Winter   171
    Reveller's and Fireside Winter   173
    The Poet's Winter   174
    God and Mary's Winter   175
    Epilogue   177
    Christmas Poem   178
    Light the Candles   179
    Life's Impossible Desire   180
    Christmas 1938   181
    Wireless   182

THE DONKEY AND THE ARK

    The Ark   185
    The Donkey Who Wouldn't Go   187
    Turn Again Dick Whittington   188

VALEDICTORY

    International Labour Office   193
    Arnold Bennett   195
    Robert Bridges   196
    Dark Rioupéroux   197
    I Drove Out from Grenoble in the Bus   198
    G. K. Chesterton   199
    Alan Davidson Keith   200

	Page
VALEDICTORY (*continued*)	
W. H. Lowe-Watson	201
Rioupéroux Re-visited	202
Gerald Gould	205
For Omar	207
Sir Arthur Steel-Maitland	208
Aristide Briand	209
George V	210
As the Starlight Exceeds	211
Death-Mask	212
Resurget Nunquam	213
Epitaph	214

OUT OF GREAT TRIBULATION

LAY your hands over these eyes. They do not wish
    to see
either the sorrow or the glory. This is he,
who has come out of great tribulation. Leave me,
    friend,
where no trumpets are sounding. I will pretend
that none of these things happened. I did not betray
the holy spirit within me. I did not pray
for ignoble victory. I did not throw down my shield
in mid-battle, and when the victors' joy-bells pealed
I did not worship at their shrines. Or if I did
I am alone by the sea now. A Nereid
rises from the waves. She does not know my name.
Girl from the waters of life, it is the same
that you heard when Achilles was slain, when the
    Romans broke
in the German marshes, and, when the centurions
    spoke
together, that name was on their lips beneath the
    Cross;
it is quiet after suffering, salvation after immortal loss;
it is fear looking in the eyes of hatred, suddenly bright;
it is a star, that time had forgotten, cracking the night;
it is God kissing the devil's brow in the depth of
    damnation.
Do not lift your hands. This is he who has come out
    of great tribulation.

A CHANT

(To be intoned on the Day of Judgment)

THIRTY pieces of silver it was that the high-priest paid
for the first Jew, the only Jew, that was by Jews
betrayed.

There were two seen on Calvary that perished by his
side,
but the third, the third was Israel, unseen and crucified.

The world is full of voices echoing the Jewish cry
" Release unto us Barabbas, but the other crucify.

Let him hang and be tortured because of his unbelief.
He shall die with the Master as we will live with the
thief."

And every night that passes an agonizing Jew
calls aloud in the churches, and the veil is rent in two.

The grave is dug and secret with none to watch and
pray,
and none to bid him rise again nor roll the stone
away.

But every night that passes the silver pieces call:
" Mills of God grind quickly, for ye grind us exceeding small."

THE NEGRO SLAVE

THIS, like a spot of light in two darknesses—
the darkness from within and the darkness from without,
this that is unquenchable, this
that is a lamp for the unknown soldier of the soul.
    " Put out
this spot of light ? "   Because of the exceeding dark—
the inward dark of the soul distraught
and the outward blackness of the desecrated ark
of the Temple ?   But these darknesses are naught.
The light is not in the poet's keeping,
nor can the darknesses embrace or estrange it.
Not any pain, nor all his desolate weeping,
nor sin nor wickedness can mar or change it.
It shines : it is not his : its unasked splendour
is his ultimate punishment.   Like a branded thief
with beauty impressed on his brow, that he cannot
    surrender
for all his prayers, he is crowned with brilliant grief.

Starred with an alien glory, like a negro slave,
who in a black sequestered hand a winter night
holds up a torch above his dead master's grave,
and breaks beneath the burden of the light—
Virginia swamps in the soul, the ganger's whip falling,
Africa breathing over his shoulder with its stale hot
    breath,
and like devils his youth betrayed, his childhood calling.
It is death, little brother, it is death.
Ah, yes, Rudyard Kipling, it is death, it is fear,
and who shall save the driven beast
when the waters disappear
and the sun smokes in the East ?
Darkness and shame and a dead negro slave,
whose withered fingers, as he crumbles, scorch,
but out of the shame, the darkness, and the grave
(witness oh crucified !) the torch.

AT THE END OF THE AVENUE

THE CHILD UNBORN

THERE is a child unborn
in the face of
all women, even the old
who have outworn
childbearing and love.
It is the tale untold
of the unslakeable thirst
dimly imagined
in the heart foredoomed to carry
unfulfilment from the first.
It is the legend
of Mary
waiting for the angel, who
cometh not at dusk
nor at morn.
In the face of all of you,
women, I see the death-mask
of a world unborn.

THE SPEARMAN

You would not have guessed nor I
how this would take the dawn and break it
in its hands.   It passes by.
It sleeps.   O, do not wake it,
lest we know again the javelin
and the smiling eyes as the shaft is prest.
Does he wake?   Does he march?   O let him in,
Let him in!   Spearman, this is my breast!

THE CYPRIOT

ALL men have said to themselves,
as daylight ended or began
in the long grasses or in the furrow,
as they hunted or took the plough by the helves
" To be a man
is to be aware of sorrow."
Shall I therefore being such, forget thee
Atropos or Norney or whatever name
was thine in service?   Shall I not
rather in the place of worship set thee
above the flame—
encircled Cypriot?
For she—the other—still is tidal,
flowing with the moon, and fled
till the gulls cry over the sands.
And he who comes as a groom to the bridal
may twist instead
the winding-sheet in his hands.
But thou to the spindle bending,
as it was planned before the years,
dost lengthen or cut the web.
Let us have done, heart, with pretending
that any tears
can draw the waters homeward when they ebb.

If I must go into the dark again,
I shall know the way without a guide.
First let the cage plunge in the mine-shaft of the heart,
in the coal-pit of the stomach,
down, down, down,
through emptiness, through terror, and with none
to wind again when the long day is done.

Thine head upon thee is like Carmel—
and the King is held in the galleries of thine hair,
with no lamp to guide him to the face.
Only the black water trickling in the six-foot tunnel,
and far-off a shrill desperate whinny
as of a pit-pony
abandoned, and left behind—
or of something else—waiting and blind.

If I must go into the dark again
among those who are benefited, being chastised,
I shall know the ways.   I shall not strike my head
against the low roof, but crouch like an animal.
I shall not think of the light for fear of madness.
I shall think only of my pick and the coal-face,
and not of that other face at all, of that face
that launched a thousand ships, and sank them
galley after galley, barquentine and bark
utterly in the dark.

" As though a violin
miraculously pure
did touch
far off the overture
of some cool thin
toccata, such
is the slender unsure
line where her breasts begin."

Under what casement who
in dream or in truth
has not, however dumb,
whispered on a sweet breath
this—as if all men knew
that love in youth
is only an air from some
song-book of Elizabeth.

" As though a violin "
(On revient toujours)
Purcell or Lawes I think
or was it Lully
weaving the motif in
" miraculously pure "—
(procul O procul hinc,
too fair to sully).

Not for the treble-lute,
the rebeck or vielle,
but where my friend Pierrot
flying from Harlequin
suddenly stricken mute,
sobbed as he fell:
" Death with my lips in snow,
just where her breasts begin."

DOWN-LEANING to thine urn
how shall I know
if thou indeed art she?
For in many shapes she doth return,
and in many go,
as it were Penelope,
as it were the daughter of Mr. Boniface,
the dealer in Morocco leather,
as it were Helen thy beauty makes me sick,
in the same window-niche, the same place
with the hands clasped together
above the tattered wick.
There were all those.   What proof
that thou art also among them,
that thou art
where Itylus beats against the roof.
And the voices, as though Ezra Pound had sung them,
are in the heart
of
Admiral Rozanoff
as his flagship went sailing, sailing,
with the Nicaeans
over the wine-dark seas
with no winds haling
into the Banzais, into the aeons,
and the waiting Japanese.
And others—Heaulmiére
the Suggéres cousin, the fair Angevine,
and the first Anne of English Harry,
the wasted hair
the brows stricken between
and the axe-blade falling, Mary.
With the hellebore petal
shadowy in thy face

dost thou return
also among these, among the fatal,
Muse or Grace
down-leaning to thine urn?

THE CALM MOUNTAIN-VALLEYS

In these calm mountain-valleys
where the snows
are benedictions anciently surmised
by one of those
who cried upon these lilies,
hugely emparadised,
" Behold! at last the Lord
by his own light adored."

I am alone with the weight of my loving.
I am come,
smaller than the shadow of that raven's wing,
not stricken dumb,
but with astonished lips scarce moving,
remembering
how in my heart she speaks
unquestioned as those peaks.

There is a place and time in the heart of lovers,
where the snows
melt not being above the line of dust.
The eagle knows
as he poises, stoops and recovers
the perfect trust
in the power to ascend
in quiet world without end.

We are alone in that place and together.
Each must find it
unhelped, and, having found it, stops,
and as the world behind it
downwards like a falling feather
quivers and drops
knows by exceeding grace
the loved one face to face.

In the mountain air candle-clean
fear and doubt
and earthly wonder and the fever
are out,
and in their place not by the senses seen,
but changing never
behold! adoring and adored
with his own splendour love the lord.

THE PAINTED FLOWER

Not the flower itself but the thought
of your flower that I have made
I have brought.
In their brief masquerade
men and the heather
put on the dominoes
of flesh and the blade's green feather.
And those
before the owl has cried
are laid aside.

But here, time overthrown,
green flame and bloom's white spark
disown
the slow atomic dark.
Division and the grief
of dust will not prevail
on bud or leaf,
nor overset the pale
but mandatory power
of an imagined flower.

The Indian conjurer
makes a bush with two passes
grow quicklier
than under sun the jungle grasses—
in momentary magic.   This
is not such: having no mortal part
nor weaknesses.
And the old fowler of the heart
can use a blossom as lime
to snare the wings of time.

AT THE END OF THE AVENUE

I HAVE walked to the end of the avenue,
and there is no figure in the clearing at the end.
It was something in the way that the trees grew:
but I shall pretend
that the evening sunlight falls on a cold
face, and touches the line of the breast
with the last level gold
out of the West.
And since I found it not in all those avenues
on all those other eves,
why should the mind refuse
what the heart believes?

TAKE then an armful of bracken
two stone-pines, a birch,
and a knoll where the grasses thicken.
There end the search!
There rest awhile and remember
(as you must, as you will)
that it is September
still
with the birch-leaves changing a little,
and the bracken folding the green arms,
which the dangerously brittle
sunshine scarce warms.
Clutch so tight to the grass
that it almost cuts, and say:
" This shall not pass
away.
This is sealed to us and we
to it, though the bracken
and the birch-tree
be stricken,
and the grass wither.
Time that plucks all
shall not gather
this small
harvest laid aside
in a world beyond
the leaf that has died
and the dead frond."
Yes ! these,
like a hill-city piled
in the distances
behind the Child
at Mary's breast, are such
as link earth's vernal
and hesitating touch
with things eternal.

LET ME BE GLAD OF PAIN

Let me be glad of pain!
Since I am caught in the flesh
why should I tremble and strain
leaping at the mesh?
I am in the body.   To-morrow
or the next day when I am free,
I shall pray in the dark for sorrow,
and it will not come to me.

THE house that I builded
has grown grey and the stones crumbled.
The rain and the storm have beaten it,
ghostly the name that was gilded,
ghostly and humbled.
For the years, the locust years, have eaten it.
The great door hangs by its hinges,
that was wide as the heel of the world,
the columns have fallen on the broad landing,
and only a sly shadow shifts and cringes
where with wings unfurled
the angels of God had room to be standing.
Yet is there one, it seems, who dwells there
in the old house, where dust like a curtain drawn
muffles the past.   I have seen light fall
as though a lover, wandered in the Hells there,
reclaimed the dawn
rocked in the dark maternal arms of nightfall.

HOW SHALL WE OVERTAKE

How shall we overtake the
thoughts that move with the horizon—
brilliant phantoms, fleeing,
with the light that dies on
their faces, irrevocably
into their own being?
Birds on the left that are
beauty's pale prophecies,
maugre
their wings, with the trail of a star
have dazzled the eyes
of the petulant augur.
He would not interpret their
flight even if he could.
For they have passed by
on their own affair,
leaving the proud solitude
of the inexplicable cry.

THE LIGHT-FOOTED

SEE! they are returning
   the light-footed ones—
The midnight grass is burning,
   as each one runs.
Swifter than torches,
   keener than knife!
O, wind in the birches
   it is love pacing life.

WHEN YOU LOOK BACK

AND later when you look back
on these first days, say, dreaming,
" Once in life that is all guesses
truth prevailed upon seeming.
Her clear high brow shone for us,
her hands were laid on our hands—
and the white birds with a sound of wings beating
soared innumerable as the sea's sands
into the eye of the sun, into the wind's sleeve
out of the dust, out of this dark, this pain.
White birds you are flighting and crying
(you will say) in my heart again."

ALWAYS you have made me to wait!
Till it seems to me now
that you would shatter
some old, immutable vow
if your gift came not later
than the most late
that I can guess.
For if I slept, and you did waken me,
mixing your breath with my breath,
I should think that you had forsaken me.
If you come before the stars pass,
Lord, you have broken faith.

THE SNOW-DICTATED PEACE

ONCE in the life of men
a light clings
about their head as though
God saw again
the swift innumerable wings
of the first snow.
As one who is wakened
to a world redrawn
by the pencil of rime
so, in that second,
dawn
escapes from time.
None can foreknow or prepare
the brilliant slender
moment of release.
It is there.
We surrender
to the snow-dictated peace.

THERE is a swallow flighting,
and a palm-tree broods in the South
under the seven
lamps that the Plough is lighting
in a strange heaven
against your mouth.
This is the mirage of trees
over the desert suspended
in green cloud-purity.
It is that unchangeable peace
of the things that cannot be,
and are not ended.

TWO OBOLS

HERE are two obols, sailor,
and let you ferry
a phantom paler
than mist in your wherry
till the black unbroken
silence defers
to the dim moth-spoken
passengers.
Pole swift up the river
to put me over
on the shore where never
again for the lover
the veils and the voices
shimmer and lift,
and the heart, that rejoices,
breaks.   Boatman, be swift!

THE COLD UNSPOKEN AND ANGRY YEARS

Swifter than the heart broken
or the end of tears,
the cold unspoken
and angry years
flood like a fistful
of tumbled bloom
through the lost, the wistful
dream-haunted room.
They fall, they settle—
shadows in the grass.
Petal by petal
they glimmer and pass.

HAIL AND FAREWELL

SONG AND SIGHT

Thus and thus I have rebuilded out of ash
what seemed to have been dustier than the dust,
as grey, as shredded, at most an irritant,
as science pretends, to fashion the core of sight.
But no! it was not so, and if I tell it—
my ash and how it was transmuted into life
not of plant, nor flower, not even of mounting bird,
but into the thought itself whence these things blossom
listen, and be persuaded!   I preach no godhead,
but in the sensible veins that feed the heart,
and carry the blood back to the thirsty skin
I have refound the secret that I had lost,
and that all lose when they begin to suffer
that lamentable truce with agony,
the long and shameful armistice that leads
to the acceptance of disgraceful peace.
So I was waiting for death without reprieve,
having lived and seeing no further goal for life;
having thought and found the edges of my mind;
having loved, and being beggared of delight.
Day follows day then with no noise or comment,
where birds resort to try their airs again,
or where the larger music of the wind
starts its wide prelude to the old sonata
that is for ever unfinished and unguessed.
A man lives solitary in a single cell
of a dessicating honeycomb, and round him
all sound, all thought, all human multitude
are drying wax, spilt wings and old dead bees.
A ray of a long-foundered sun or moon
may regild or resilver for an instant
a day forgotten, or spring may re-embody,
most fleetingly, a presence or a shape,
in which our soul was dressed—a boy perhaps
seeing his first mountain—oh the white, white peak,
and the great bastions scrawling at the skies

with elemental firs, nature's green monks
that tell their beads, climbing with forehead bowed
in the eternal progress of the Host.
But that's as painful as brief, and, as Time coats
the soul with deeper dust, more rarely comes.
So that for me at least there were no changes
in the long rust, but only the wind stirring
the powdered days and the deciduous nights,
and the small crackle of thorns too blunt to wound.
Safety! Yes, I had that—as the least blade
so near the earth not even a foot can crush it,
and naught to see save the next neighbouring stem,
and naught to feel but the slowly ageing sap.
And then it was I heard one singing again!
Forgive me, God, if I call on your Name,
or make a God for a name great enough
to qualify that singing and that song.
No! not the thing she said, but she who said it
and how 'twas said. Of all created flowers
lilac is nearest the dew. If asphodel—
the legendary sort—had from the meadows
beyond the stars in April been transplanted,
it would have bloomed upon a lilac tree,
because the lilac in its trembling arms
enfolds the brief eternity of youth
defeating death with its bright alibi.
Well then! she was the lilac-asphodel
in poignant loveliness and quiet awe
breathing upon the ruins with the fragrance
of the larger meads under dream-Tyrian skies.
And this she sang, or rather in her being
scent, light, and youth, framed in unspoken words,
were cool and audible as imagined rain!

" There are dead planets that keep their bright patrol,
    ringed before Saturn, more flagrant once than Mars,
dark now as Lucifer's dipped aureole,
    fallen yet sensible between the stars.

These shouldered time away, or sought to curb it,
  holding his horses in dream's shadowy rein,
bidding his stallions swing into the orbit
  where joy upon itself returns again.

But they are fallen into darkness, these proud,
  there is none to do them honour in all the skies.
But O forgotten, O great with your heads bowed,
  be patient still.   For you have great allies.

Time, leaning backwards, folds you to its breast,
  your scattered dawns are gathered out of space,
their grey and gold consummate and at rest,
  seeing the Dawn they sprang from face to face.

And so all love, and so our life in death,
  go all in splendour, and in darkness end,
but there is one whose heart remembereth,
  who is enriched for ever by what they spend."

I have laid the dawn away. I have estranged the
      noon.
Come quickly night of stars or starless.   I am ready
for darkness.   I shall hear her in the dark.

THE EASTERN WELL

YOUR young head is set upon your shoulders
as though the Italian sculptor who designed you,
carrying your pitcher to the well of life,
had by a trick set the dim East behind you.

But I a stranger, waiting at the well-head,
returning from the long pilgrimage of years,
cannot divine the meaning of your laughter,
and dare not divine the challenge of your tears.

I, looking back through time as you draw nearer,
somnambulist in the lost paradise
of dreams dew-footed that I had forgotten,
watch my own youth ascendant in your eyes.

But not for me thus gazing to unriddle
the movement of your hand and your flushed cheek,
and the unspoken, lovelier overtone
behind the half-remembered words you speak.

Go back from the well! I cannot fill your pitcher
with any water save from the fountains of grief.
Go back from the well! And—see—I break the
    lutestrings,
lest you should stay and I become love's thief.

LIEBESTOD

Is it cool at the heart of music?   Is it hushed
   when the waves ripple out from the motionless
      centre?
Dark as the wine unborn before the grape is crushed,
   and tense as the empty stage before the actors enter?

If it be so, and since you came to my life so laggard,
   so late, Tristran, leave me a moment's grace,
lest I should seem old, broken and haggard
   when I look upward trembling into your face.

Leave me with the quiet, Tristran.   It seemed too late
   to be reborn in beauty, to suffer the brilliant thrust
of first love in the Autumn.   Beloved! wait,
   and let me write with a finger in the dust.

I shall look up presently.   Now let me hear you
   singing, with my head bent, scarce drawing breath.
Sweet, I shall never again be so utterly near you.
   For the beginning of love is the beginning of death.

A PRAYER

Now you lay your head to rest,
        loveliest.
And I need not pray for you
        morning-dew,
knowing, sweet, that you will waken
        the breast shaken,
and your lips in wonder parted
as they were when love first started.

THE STONE GOD

SEEING you a man might have been puzzled
    with an old race-memory
of a dim temple dazzled
    by a goddess from the sea,

and of how the old grey god that had crumbled
    through Time, like a frozen breath,
knew her, and his stone lips trembled
    between love and his own death.

So, seeing you, a man might have cried
    on the goddess that his heart had known
in the temple, where he had suffered and died,
    a time-wasted god of stone.

THE WOOD NYMPH SPEAKS

MAKE me not to remember the reed,
    nor use me cruelly, being estranged,
for reed-music.   Subdue your lovely greed
    lest the hoof be cloven, the heart changed.

I can run lightly on bare feet,
    treading no thorn between the mosses.
Let you be gentle while I am fleet,
    let it still be the time of primroses,

cool against the cheek, cool in the breast.
    O ! let there be nor asking nor taking.
Let it be evening at quietest,
    let it be dream and not waking.

THE CORINTHIAN GARLANDS

It is unimportant, Anthony, that my breast is stone.
The Corinthian garlands do not wither like the bay.
If I had been flesh and blood I should not have known
how the ivy clings and bites nearer day by day.

There is a statue Pheidias broke with his maul:
O the breast of stone, O the inviolate breast!
Is it unimportant, Anthony, after all
of the women you loved to have been the quietest?

At the end of the garden, at the shadow's end
they will dig the grave for you, and break your zither.
Sleep with your music, Anthony, sleep softly, friend!
For only the Corinthian garlands do not wither.

EXTREME DIAMOND

FOR longer than you guess
I have been watching your face
until its loveliness
fades upon space.

Distant, unrequited, cold
it glimmers beyond
nights manifold
an extreme diamond.

But who can recover the trace
of the snowflake in the snow?
I have been watching your face
from further than you know.

THE GARDENIA

WEAR this gardenia
  against your heart to hide it,
and if the sister flower
  should softly chide it
for that great modesty
  in being hid,
answer, as under wave
  a Nereid
might to the dappled moon:
  "You do but shine
with light reflected, but
  this heart of mine
has her own flame and is, beside,
  the sun
that floods the darkness
  of another one."

A VOW

For inasmuch as by strange paths the blood
    flows, and so ebbs, none knowing how,
let us, who cannot check this traveller,
    take for ourselves a vow.

As sweetly as it has borne us to this goal,
    so trusting to its secret wisdom, we
shall make no question of its windings
    to what or to no sea.

We have been greatly moved from its far springs,
    admitted to its morning utterance.
We will not ask at afternoon or evening
    whither it bears us hence.

Many must die who never knew love's name,
    and more who only used him as a stranger;
with us familiar, we will walk with him
    gladly from danger into danger.

HE ASKS A PROMISE

Give me this promise! To be never
　　the same. Or rather swear
it shall not be this evening on this river,
　　　　and I not there.

Look not, if you must look, thus stricken,
　　midnight on your lips, nor close
your eyes against the light when new lights quicken,
　　　　and my light goes.

Give me this promise, that hereafter,
　　whatever may be lost along the years,
no one but I will ever hear this laughter,
　　　　nor stanch these tears.

EXODUS

SHE will not look back; the strange faring
divides and estranges. She goes, it seems,
into her own distance, bearing
the weight of unshared dreams.

So a Jewish woman left her Nile
for Canaan and the garden-plots,
head up, but listened all the while
for the reclaiming chariots.

YOU MUST NOT ASK

You must not ask
    that in my middle years
I'll pluck the stars
    for jewels at your ears.

You must not think
    that I will rob the West
to hang the sun's disaster
    at your breast.

You must not hope
    that for a kiss I'll squander
death for your coronation,
    like Leander.

I do but offer
    the quiet aftermath
of eve descending
    on a forest path.

I do but bring
    these cold, these dim, these pale
cadences of the
    tired nightingale.

And when you hear
    between the branches
a voice that storms
    the night with painful inches

say in your heart,
  "You might have sung,
Helene, Ronsard,
  had you, like her, been young."

THE DESERTED GOD

Was it long since you listened
  to that music, and by what dim pool,
did you see the face of your first belovéd
  desperately beautiful?

Nay do not tell me!   I shall remember
  by mere agony what I could not have known—
unless there were a third unnoticed—
  a garden-god of stone.

Yes I was stone—and you the living lovers,
  and the moon's indiscriminate grace
marbles your kisses as she discovers
  life in the motionless face.

First love, young love, and then the dew returning
  to the place where your feet had trod,
and the sound of your voices dying—
  and the deserted garden-god.

DISPOSSESSION

I MAY have lost you.   Should I care
when every day and everywhere
the things that we believed we were
grow, by omission, lovelier.
The loss is present where your face
composed the lassitude of space,
or lips, despite his ancient treason,
with a kiss conquered time for reason.
But present loss is absent gain
as heart, instructed by the brain,
dismisses shadows on a blind
of the light burning in the mind.
And if the untransmuted hunger
regrets the sweets it tastes no longer—
no more to breathe each other's sighs,
when love of mere fulfilment dies,
no more to give, no more to take
the light in whose immortal wake
the bubble darkness of the grave
dives coloured in the coloured wave—
we know it for a lovely cheat—
its own demand its own defeat—
that always seeks and always loses
the truth its own desire confuses.
No! let us live as though in bronze
we moulded what our love was once,
with maul and chisel lending form
to what, because it is not warm,
has the smooth peace, the carvéd grace
of statues in the market-place—
for all to see and all to share
the love that is no longer there.

THE FLOWER

I wish that you had given me a flower.
  I would have said to the years: " Yes! you are fleet!
But in my heart, beyond your utmost power,
  this will be fresh for ever, and be sweet."

Why should we care for things the hand can hold?
  Memory should be enough.   Yet all night through
a single flower, one English marigold,
  hung in the air between my love and you.

It is raining on the roofs, and in my heart,
  grey refugees, the scattered rain-clouds cower.
I did not know, that when we came to part,
  there could have been such virtue in a flower.

RED SHOES

Wear your red shoes as once
on such a night, as deep
with blue or bronze
a dark Venetian lady
wore such red shoes.
And that great use
has made your red shoes seem
as though love danced in them
wearing the silken mask,
the flowered domino.
Wear them because I ask—
and when I go.

THE BLUE GODDESS

I BRING no excuse, but out of the remote days
   the figure of the blue goddess that you know.
Other things alter and go their inconstant ways,
   but she is constant and she does not go.

It is not because of the stone in which they carved her
   that she is resolute where all else falters.
It is because they have forgotten and starved her
   in all her temples and by her fallen altars.

Greater than her sorrow, as she surpassed her praise,
   she learns in disgrace, what never the half-gods know,
that love, desire and beauty go their ways,
   but the heart in its own possession does not go.

NIGHTINGALE-THROATED

Look! it is only a crumpled pellet the flower that I took,
  and yet all night it has haunted me with its scent.
If you could do this much with a petalled hook,
  what will you do when the hook is threaded and bent?

What will you do when the argent fish has floated
  out of its cool stream between the grasses and reeds?
And what will you answer, O nightingale-throated,
  when love and not song is the water that he needs?

It is easy, sweet angler, to fish by the stream,
  and to draw in the rod with its glittering prize.
But if you have landed the silver of dream
  what will you do when you open your eyes?

RETURN

Come back! You were mistaken!
   This is the true dawn.
It is the lilac, not the bracken
   greening on ledge and lawn.

Lift your heavy head from the pillow,
   and let your ears be learning
that cry is not the last swallow
   but the first returning.

Come out in mourning not arrayed,
   but under this tidal
impulse of spring, come as a maid
   robed for her bridal.

Come back! For doubts, their conquest meagre,
   disowned fly each from each!
Come back! For time has raised his leaguer,
   and love is through the breach.

ALL BUT FALLEN CITY

I FOUND these flowers on the dark borders.
   I have brought them back as I came,
and you alone, keeper of my lost garden,
   can tell me what is their sunlit name.

They have the look of those other flowers
   that grew in the day's eye and their scent.
But it may be that they are only shadows,
   cast by the others when they went.

It may be that these Autumn roses
   are not mine to bring, nor yours to take.
It may be that I must return to the border
   by the dim waters of the shoreless lake.

Or it may be that you will name them,
   sounding, through the cordon of grief,
in my all but fallen city
      the trumpets of relief.

THE RIB OF ADAM

WHEN I come back to you
   wounded and afraid
out of the darkness that
   my fears have made,

and the shadow walks with me,
   but always faster,
like the great servant of
   a less master,

no arch of triumph
   no flag, no wreath
welcomes the traveller
   home from death.

But silence gathers,
   belovèd, deep
as when, in Paradisal
   sleep

out of the living
   flesh of man
out of his agony
   love began.

I'LL not be silent, never fear me, sweet
   but rhyming in the place they set apart
for fools who died of love, I'll hear your feet
   so far, so soft, they will not hurt my heart.

And one bright fool, as they in distance die,
   will say, " I thought she loved me, and was wrong,"
and " Be at peace," his fellow will reply,
   " For only to remember here is song."

Nor need your later love, by me misled,
   poison the kisses with a vain regret.
I was not living and I am not dead,
   who, then forgotten, do not now forget.

Do not forget, and need not, since all this—
   all love, all consummation, all desire
will not be mine nor yours, nor yours and his,
   but flame that burns with untranslated fire.

I PRAISE OTHER WOMEN

I PRAISE other women in you,
not the ladies of legend but
the quiet ones,
the innumerable cohort, who
have heard the gates shut
behind their love or their sons,
and go steadfast on their ways.
These women, praising you, I praise.

DEAR vulnerable face, whose wounds reclaim
   all that still grieves
in the desperate name
   of legendary loves, look up through leaves!

The latticed sky with green renews its tryst,
   as when through trees
Abelard watched the shadow of his Christ
   fall about Heloise.

Be comforted with what surpasses grief,
   with sorrow's mere excess;
and see! I bring of all those leaves this leaf.
   Keep it. Death will not guess.

QUESTIONS AND NO ANSWERS

LIGHT BALANCES

LIGHT balances only on light
but the dark is in your eyes and on your heart.
Those who were born with sight
stand apart.

The sun is intolerable to these;
the least of the stars
leaves on their eyelashes
incurable scars.

This is their pain and their reward.
They are swift and they cannot move.
Those who live by your sword,
light, must perish thereof.

Iᴛ is a long time since you went away from me,
and I have not tried in all that time to find you.
I was afraid that you should find me how altered!
But I had not believed that absence could blind you.

You grope with your hands, who walked once like a
     Greek girl
carrying an amphora poised on a proud young shoulder.
You are silent, whose voice was a mountain-torrent,
as fresh, as clear, and with dreams untravelled colder.

It was a long time since you went away, old blind
     woman,
but hear me in your darkness, Euterpe, if you can.
There was a boy once shouted your name at Vallom-
     brosa
when the leaves scattered. Feel to his forehead. He
     is a blind old man.

MY THOUGHT

LET her suppose—the hare in the underwood,
that she will run through the shade and not be caught.
And let you suppose that you also could
escape through the snares of darkness, my thought.

Course through the moss, by the hedge, in the furrow,
fly swift and soft as the shadow of a sound:
at the end of the flight is the hunter—sorrow,
and here—at your throat—the nameless hound.

MONK OF THE HEART

Monk of the heart, with forehead bowed
    under love's consecrating hand,
teach us, since we are also vowed,
    to sacrifice and understand.

For thee our days are but a whisper
    between the matin-bell and some
anticipated chime of vesper
    that calls the wanderer home.

The void of space for thee is less
    than thy cell's humble girth,
whose continental loveliness
    holds the peace of all the earth.

We cannot find thee, eremite,
    thou selfless vision, dream withdrawn,
and yet thou art in all our night
    the certain promise of the dawn.

THE YELLOW ROSE

Why should a bud
no more than a tossed cream have that pale power
to make a twilit garden of the blood
      and all the heart a flower?

Foam-silk apparelled
with trumpet faint, blown for an unseen master,
in the hushed lists of the soul it sounds, dim herald,
      the prelude of disaster.

All fair, all fond
(that tucket thrills) is but a flag unfurled
to the cold mountain-wind that blows beyond
      this bright and Persian world.

It is a tale
that ends with the first phrase, low as the changes
of bells far-off, or the late nightingale
      whose throat the year estranges.

Nay! ask not why
this brief, this blonde outpoints our life.   Who knows
if, where in dark death's crimson petals lie,
      love tends his yellow rose.

VICTORIA

The Lost Leave-Trains

THEY are slipping out into the night
    with screened windows and no sound—
one red light and another red light,
    clear in the dark like a wound.

They go, as they used to go, terribly
    dragging the heart with the red
light, that dimmed eyes could barely see,
    and with the murmur of last words said.

They are " Good-bye," they are " Come back,"
    they are " All I had I gave." . . .
They are silently slipping into the black
    in the way that they used to have.

THE BELLRINGERS

Across the further field
  bells, dimly pealed,
what evening fancy stirs
  the bellringers?

Before you called so still
  brooded my hill,
I almost heard the cloud
  rustle aloud.

It was so quiet I
  heard life pass by
(O were your voices hers,
  far bellringers?)

As though on the pale coast
  of dream, her ghost
murmured (and passed in slumber)
  snow-soft, " Remember! "

Snow-bright as climbing swan
  the dream was gone,
and as imagined verse
  fair, bellringers.

The heart, thus guided, spells
  your bright script, bells,
enriches and estranges
  with loss, your changes.

Life passed with evening as
our world must pass,
as you and love and verse—
all bellringers.

DIMENSIONAL

WE have tried this in three ways.
(What are the three dimensions called?   Birth,
marriage and death?)   Well what of the fourth?
What is the charade that the sunflower plays
with her splay green foot in the earth
and her heart for ever denying the comfortable North?
What is the use, tall stranger, of your South,
you cannot reach it however your gilded circle
twists with that distant, unconvincing star.
Better accept the bee that grumbles at your mouth,
better be groundling and obediently sparkle
humbly in greeting to your uncelestial Lar—
the little god of the gardens, who never plunges
into the formless sky, who does not ravish
clouds with his pirate stem, who does not claim
that his gold claws are in the perilous flanges
of the brazen doors of worship.   Be slavish,
sunflower; take a new and earthly name.
Still we have tried three ways.   The fourth defies us.
Though the brain burst, though the heart split asunder
shall we be patient?   Shall we stand idle?
The little soul—our timid shadow—denies us.
We will deny our soul, and, slipping under,
flow out into the darkness that is tidal.

Lay aside phrases; speak as in the night
a child in terror might.
Confess that you are lonely, that you heard
some foot or hand that stirred,
that, holding your own breath, you almost hear
the midnight breath of Fear,
that tearless, soundless in your heart you pray:
" God! give me back the day! "
Yes! God can give it back, but not the one
that you have dreamed upon.
The black will turn to grey, the grey to blue
distance, but not for you,
and not for you the cheerful voice of men
will warm your heart again.
Nor will your friends or enemies intrude
upon that solitude,
where only shadows drift and cross and pass,
seen sideways in your glass.
Make not complaint. For neither prayer nor tear
has its old power here.
This is not silence rounded by the deep
deliverance of sleep,
but by the empty spaces where the will
to wake again is still.
You chose, and you abide the choice, apart,
saying to your own heart:
" Beat if you must, though softly," to the brain,
" Must you imagine pain? "
And last of all say to the sobbing breath:
" No, fool, this is not death."

PURGATION

If failure is a purgation
that burns the gold and leaves the dross,
mine is the proud, ultimate
conviction by loss.

I should be able to speak truly
for all those who have wearily come
to the purposeless end of the road
stale, helpless, dumb.

I should have the accent
of the feet that drag and thrust
in the monotonous futile
passage from dust to dust.

There should be a fraudulent echo
of a beautiful lying tongue,
a wisp of sweet false roses
with their roots in dung.

So that a man or woman reading
may curse it for sad stuff,
because it is their own unvarnished story,
and that will be enough.

GENTLY AS THE GRASS GROWS

GENTLY as the grass grows
     the grass flaws,
it comes and goes
     by the same quiet laws
     (no lesser and no greater)
     than dug Mount Etna's crater.

Swiftly as the bird flies
     the bird tumbles,
it lives and dies
     it sings and crumbles
     by the same rule,
     mercilessly merciful.

Sweetly as the cheek flushes
     the cheek pales
blood beats and hushes,
     it flows and fails
     by the same fiat
     that the stars die at.

And these that are my hands
     yours clasping,
shift like sea-sands
     with the sea rasping,
     and the lips I kiss
     wear dust's warm liveries.

THE LAUNCH

Look down the slipway! The launched ship will not
  return.
  For good or ill the makers have done. Let her
  waken,
let her be herself, let her suffer, let her learn
  that the spirit is not given, but is painfully taken.

Let her head for the sea. They cannot save her—
  the rivetters, the shipwrights, the platers, the caulkers.
She must use as she can, the strength that they gave her.
  She will walk alone now with the sea's cold walkers.

The slipway is empty. She goes to her marriage
  with danger—the difficult bridegroom. God send her
the cold high forehead, the grey-eyed courage
  that none but her own adventure can lend her.

The first wave has lapped at her keel. She is ours no
  more.
  She belongs to the sea, to herself and to that foredoomed meeting
with the end that the first hammer-stroke fashioned her
  for.
  Head for the baths of the sun, wanderer! Farewell—
  and greeting.

SPRING

HEART, be not hurt by daffodils reborn
in the same shape in which youth also died,
nor by that bird upon whose tiny thorn
remembered love is crucified.

Nor, heart, be wrung by desperate loveliness,
nor by the hopeless rapture of the ear.
For those who see, and listen, and do not guess—
for the unwounded—hoard your selfish tear.

INVIOLATE STRANGER

I SHALL remember how slow the evening came,
  how long the daylight waited, and cry aloud,
as would a king, giving a knight his new name,
  " Rise thou, gold spurrèd midnight, and be proud "

Inviolate stranger, riding to what dark war,
  paused you beside the inn at which I lay,
and knocked against the shutter, and did no more
  than look upon my face and ride away.

No more! What more was needed? Since I mounted
  a darker palfrey even than your own,
and, long before the dawn your stars discounted,
  had ridden out for ever, and not alone.

LET not your heart by instancy affrighted
   the stroke of love abash
born, suffered, and requited
   in one star-lightning flash.

No! rather think that we were given
   the countersign and key
of his immediate heaven
   immediately,

that without asking why or whither
   he beckoned, nor how he came,
we have stepped suddenly together
   naked into the flame.

TROY

THUS shall her hair be secret with the dangers
of nights, when Helen on the walls of Troy
let down such hair, and watched the moon's cold fingers
clap the white throat of some dead Argive boy.

For we are taken in nets that fishermen
cast in Scamander and slow Simois
between the legendary battles, when,
Achilles forgotten, they spoke of that and this,

as is the way of men, of wife, of farm,
of what birds come to Argos in the spring,
of children, when their tired heads lie warm
on pillow, and indeed of anything,

that is the stuff of life.   And they would lie
easily by the river, till one would fill in
the sudden quiet with a deep-throated, " Why? "
and in their eyes the fabled face of Helen

would glitter, and each would see her, and turn aside
lest each should be betrayed, and let them guess
that cheated hopes, loves lost, and dreams denied
were little enough to fan that loveliness.

And when its flame faded in their eyes, they went,
leaving their nets, to battle, and some were slain,
and some grew old and died, but all were spent
at the last, and corn grows on the Trojan plain.

We do not know their names, but even as they,
whether battle-weary they died or fighting fell,
finding our Helen in the belovèd say,
though all is lost and the heart breaks, " It is well."

PARTS OF SPEECH

THE history of parts of speech—
First jagged flints on time's long beach:
then smoothed and used by wave and tide,
with long attrition unified,
they stir together with the single
rustle of sea-distracted shingle,
fused but not yet organic.   Next
with radiant agony perplext
sway as with sap, and greenly slant
with the dim pulses of a plant.
Thence groping tendrils shift and climb
along the temple-walls of time
till those dark movements change their heat,
and with a swifter cadence beat
in upward strife through fish and ape,
dumbly conniving at escape
into the muted light where strings
make waves of words, and thoughts of things.
And, though imperfect, now acquainted
with what on earth was never minted,
but comes from far, and makes of them
the breath, the vision and the dream.

PIERROT AGAIN

THERE is no need to be ashamed, Pierrot,
   that you are pale and restless and cannot stay,
and that your voice is faint as a white flower;
     that is the moon's way.

There is no need to hide your hands, Pierrot;
   we would not hold you even by the long sleeves:
for they are the tobacco-plant foaming over
     on lost midsummer eves.

There is no need to pretend or answer, Pierrot.
   For we will remember Endymion,
and how he awakened pale on the mountain,
     and the moon was gone.

THE MASK

WHEN the mask is rejected
and hung on the Juggler's string,
then the unsuspected
face will be wakening.

Timid with shifting features
and eyes that, a random hole
let in a surgeon's sutures,
vaguely suggest a soul.

And there will be no soul, brother,
but only in the dusk,
faintly discerned, another
and more sardonic mask.

G

MERLIN it was who wrote in the first chapter
of Arthur's book, to the dim sound
of the Grey Women spinning in the gloom:
" It will be lonely with the sceptre,
it will not be easy to walk crowned,
nor light to carry a people's doom."

It is lonely with the sceptre, magician!
Fellowship for all others of their kind,
and equal hands to take an equal part.
But who can modify the king's vision,
who be at company in the king's mind,
or be at rest in that unresting heart?

It is not easy, wizard, to walk crowned.
The sword, the pen, the hammer all must tremble,
and even the mitre has its earthly measure.
But this is not by any limit bound,
whose only use is to be life's sleepless symbol,
whose only ease is death's exceeding leisure.

It is not light to carry a people's doom—
a heavy barge, a dark flood to ferry—
in every subject to die a separate death—
ah wherefore suffer so, for what, for whom?
How do you say, great Edward, Tudor Harry,
and you, when the ships sailed, Elizabeth?

" We chose not: we were chosen. Elect of pain
by power to endure till the breath dwindled,
the footing foundered and the heart frozen—
our blotted lanterns in her sun rekindled
England—who bade us serve her, not in vain."
King George of England, you were also chosen.

CORONATION

This is not a new crown.   Harold the Saxon wore it.
William from overseas assumed it, when the arrow
put out the Saxon light; kings of the Broom
made half of France in battle bend before it.
Rose-blood welded its stones, and in the narrow
seas Gloriana gave it the world for room.

It was a king's crown first.   Now its vast orbit
has the gold stations of a star ascending,
as dawn to dawn it diadems the earth.
What power of foe or destiny shall curb it,
how shall it fear a swift or temporal ending,
if it be worn worthily of its own worth?

Men speak of freedom now, as of a weakness
that cowards use as refuge from the forces
of the sword—the ensign of heroic youth.
But when the swords are out, and the old bleakness
of hate returns, then in her established courses
freedom stands up, the last ally of truth.

This crown is aneled of freedom; it is a token
of man's enfranchisement.   Yes! it has faltered
as all things mortal must; has erred; has failed.
And yet, when at the last, sentence is spoken,
it will remain unshaken and unaltered—
the light that over darkness has prevailed.

They will lift it on high, King George, before it is laid
upon your head, and in the hush around you
you will almost hear far voices whispering
of the old kings who watch; " Be not afraid!
We too were bound by the symbol that has bound you,
whose service is perfect freedom.   Accept it, King."

PLACES

A SONG OF COMPASSES

I AM weary of the North.
(Bend needle of the earth!
Be thou unfaithful!   Swing
out of true reckoning.)
Not South!   I do not ask
for the dim tamarisk
lit with star-weary lies
of heavenly fireflies,
so fair, so brief, so false,
as a drowned peal of bells.
Nor point me to the East—
that lotus-fingered priest,
who charms with that slow scent
the drowsy firmament.
O not for these, or this,
set, earth, your compasses,
but shatter, and be at rest
where East lies down with West.

THERE is an old loom, an old warp and woof,
older than the knitting fingers of the roaring machine,
  older
than the bales of cloth ranged in the dim warehouses.
This loom had the unstained blue of heaven for its
  roof;
it wove with the trees from shoulder to sturdy shoulder
of the great moors and made its pattern of this.

This was the first loom. It had the cry of the birds
  in it,
the curlews that have the sorrow in their thin high
  voices;
it had the whisper of the beck, and the quiet talk of
  shepherds.
It was long as the centuries, passionate as love's minute,
when the sun in the gilded cornfields walks and rejoices,
or when the claws of the rain pounce with the leap of
  leopards.

There is the second loom. This was of man's making,
his stubborn answer to the beauty he cannot control,
his answer to want, to the earth that mocks and
  defies him.
The clear swift waters of the beck are lost or defiled,
no little wind in the branches softly beseeches
the grace of dawn, and the sheep-bells are no longer
  heard.

So much the loom has destroyed, so much has it
  altered.
But one thing remains, the untamed spirit of those
who fought for Cromwell, and who died alone in the
  storm

saving their sheep.   It has not wavered nor faltered
since the tabarded days of the white and regnant rose,
since the shepherd carried the lamb, little, and close,
    and warm.

These are the Bradford men.   They are not smooth
    nor gracious;
they have no tricks of manner nor ways to flatter;
they are not swift of fashion nor easy to bend.
But the heart within them as their own moors is
    spacious,
their hands are not bowed and they go; and it will
    not matter
what danger opposes or threatens, they go to the end.

LABOR OMNIA VINCIT

I

AND labour conquers all.   Like great green cattle
   the moors browse under a sky with never a fleck.
No sound save curlews crying and the tattle,
      between her water-meadows, of the beck.
So quiet it is you almost hear the rattle
      of the mare's harness at the sudden check,
when the one horseman, riding home from battle,
      silently drops the reins upon her neck,
and gazes steadily upon the valley,
      the drowsing pastures, and the homely stream,
      nor guesses, as he slips the stirrups down,
that the black outlines mixing casually
      with night are the long shadows in a dream,
      cast by the unborn streets of Bradford town.

II

Where lies true beauty?   William Wordsworth rated
   the first steam-engine that surprised Winander,
while Turner with his coloured carbons stated
   speed in bright terms of enigmatic splendour.
The evenglow tranquil on trees belated
   persuades the weary spirit to surrender
to the hushed charm, not in the mind created,
   of borderlands where reason yields to wonder.
These are green benedictions freely proffered
   by God or nature,—His elected vicar,
   to those who worship in His chapel of ease,
Yet there are Masses to the vision offered
   no differently, when the tall candles flicker
   in other and laborious services.

III

Here is the ridge on which the horseman pondered,
  there is the valley, there the hidden stream,
and there, for all the changes, still unsquandered
  the secret architecture of the dream.
Nor ask if mankind, from God's purpose wandered,
  following a faithless star, have hitched their team
not to its gold in heaven but to the plundered
  false beacons of some Jack-o-lanthorn gleam.
There is no answer.   Here are brick and stone,
  the loud machine, the vext industrious days,
  wearing their squalor like a mill-girl's shawl.
But, like that horseman, when we ride out alone
    looking our last, we also may pause, and praise,
    because we have learned that labour conquers all.

THERE was a boy.   The little mists around him
  flicker and change.   I cannot see him clear.
And yet, although I seek, and have not found him,
  nothing so certainly as he is here.

His eyes are deep with knowledge not his own,
  his lips with retrospective sorrow dim.
For the cries of all the years he has not known
  strain through my shadow, and encompass him.

He listens to a wandered sound that baffles
  the bells of youth, and sees the first flush spent
in life's indifferent radiance, that muffles
  with the full day the dawn's astonishment.

Behind him fades his father's house he came from,
  already with remembrance pitiful,
and the school, that he must enter, takes its name from
  an older, and a darker, Grammar School.

He stands between his childhood and his age,
  between this shadow and that further shade,
but, like all men, he has for heritage
  the truth and beauty other men have made.

Rich with their labour, with their thought anointed,
  heir to their anguish, with their love requited,
he passes by the road their lives have pointed
  under the constellations they have lighted.

There is no victory but they have shaped it,
　　no glory but they knew it, and no fame—
no gold memorial—but they have draped it
　　with the tall flags of their unwritten name.

Who is the boy? I cannot see him plain.
　　The mists return, and yet, before they hide him
for ever, let us look on him again,
　　and set that last grave memory beside him.

Look back, and know that he has seen us too,
　　that we are one with him, and life is thus
not I alone, nor you, and you, and you,
　　but what our fathers were, and all of us.

THE hunt is up at Porlock and the hounds are well away.
  (Satan, are you sleeping there below?)
The gulls with breasts gold-dusted string out across
    the bay
  and the moorland is a brazier burning slow.
The sky is like a bonfire with the flames all blue,
  and the clouds like a whisper in the snow.
And the world is like a blessing, with the hunt at
    Minehead guessing
  it's a perfect day for slaughter, and by God! they
    ought to know.

Hounds are in the Devon hills, beside the Devon seas,
  (Satan, are you sleeping there below?)
The gallant hunt at Minehead are riding at their ease
  wondering when a stag will show.
" Tell the men of England, tell 'em clear and true
  how the hunt at Minehead told you so,
That God is in his heaven, and it seems to men in Devon
  a perfect day for slaughter, and by God! they
    ought to know."

The stag's asleep in covert,—brow, bay and tray, and
    three.
  (Satan, are you sleeping there below?)
But they've got a hind they've tufted, and they've run
    her to the sea
  and she's swimming all the way to Plymouth Hoe.
Get out the launches and man the motor-craft,
  as the life-boat seems too slow,
and if hounds have torn her throat, or she is run down
    by a motor,
  it's all the same at Minehead, and by God! they
    ought to know.

Drake he's in his hammock till the great Armadas
    come
    (Satan, are you sleeping there below?)
But it seems to me that Minehead must have heard his
    drum
    when they gave the hind to hounds with a throw:
" I loved the whole of England, but most of all the red
    cliffs where the best of England grow.
But if these be men of Devon, I'll quit the port of heaven,
    and I'll drum them down the Channel, and by God!
        they ought to go."

HOLLINGS HILL

LAST year (a hundred years ago?)
   I walked up Hollings Hill.
I do not know (does any know?)
   if it is climbing still
out of the clatter, out of smoke
   into a quiet place,
where all that cracked or flawed or broke
   resumes its ancient grace,
where with the curlews highly calling,
   and the wind upon the heath,
the benisons of youth are falling
   upon the world beneath,
till ruined hearts, that life has nailed on
   the Cross of their own making,
are lifted down where over Baildon
   the dawn is re-awaking.
Last year (a hundred years ago)
   I heard on Hollings Hill
a world of larks.   Does any know
   if they are singing still?

ABERUCHIL

I WILL offer you the best that I have—
a walled garden enclosed within the hills.
It is a deep and ancient turf,
but the flowers have stormed the walls in a wave
till it seems that the last of the roses spills
at the foot of the pines in coloured surf.

Other men in a vexed world offer their pain,
bringing defeat and ugliness as a gift,
unwilling to love and unable to pardon.
But I have come home to the hills again,
and I offer the flowers that heap and drift
to the flowerless world out of my garden.

It is mine to give because I can snare it,
where the shadow has fallen, the fragrance lingers
in this handful of words that my heart has strung.
It is a charm against sorrow.   Wear it,
and quiet will touch you with cool far fingers
because you have listened and I have sung.

VENICE

VENICE—and the gondola floating on
 (she whispers) with bubbles like silver pennies,
rustling about the breast of a swan,
 and you with your boating-straw in Venice.

So to eternity floating together
 you cock your colours over your eyes,
and it's always evening and summer weather,
 and romance for ever before us flies!

You little fellow, who with a mouthful
 snared me of lovely glittering words,
what a goose you are in the drowsy South full
 of men as secret and wild as birds!

They have flown past us while you lie sleeping;
 they look back at me with vivid deep
eyes so strange that I should be weeping,
 and thanking God that I still can weep.

Venice—and the Gondola floating through
 the Grand Canal, and you not a man
but only a little singing Jew
 that netted the soul of a Christian.

Gondolier leave the boat.   So! clear her!
 Whither?   Why ask me?   You are paid:
and, if beyond the bar I steer her,
 why fear—if I am not afraid?

ASHFORD CHACE

Here is the perfect place to be,
whose absolute tranquillity
is such a single breath of scent
from thyme seems almost violent.
Flowers without in lace or hoop,
with scarf of gold or silver loop
storm at the doors, as if to win
acquaintance with their quiet kin—
the books that, fragrant as themselves,
make a rose-garden of the shelves.

Far skyline over lawn and rill
as you are still, let this be still
always! As though beside the wells
of ancient peace, green sentinels—
your vigilant trees—let nothing pass
except the shadows on the grass,
whose only function is to give
peace her withdrawn superlative.

Always be quiet: always be
the image of that time, when we
and God with nothing yet to pardon
in one another, shared a garden.

ICELAND

In that cold land where slow dawns clamber
hardly through the shadow, did you guess
how the trees were losing in England
for want of coolness and of you their green?
Or did you remember
only how in her loveliness
we saw with all her leaves a plane-tree stand
in the summers that have been?

ANOTHER WAY

THERE is another way past the brickyard
    past the board school playground and the petrol
        pumps.
You turn by the end of the electric tram-lines,
    between the gasometer and the municipal dumps.

No need to change your ready-made trousers,
    nor wash your celluloid collar, nor trouble
to adjust your slouch, nor straighten your shoulders,
    nor lift your working boots high over the rubble.

There is another way and a woman to walk with.
    See, she points over her shoulder with her thumb.
She looks like a portrait of someone in the papers,
    but don't bother about that or anything, only come!

Those patches on the left are market-gardens,
    advertisements, no doubt, of Mutton's seeds,
and on the right those lawns laid with green damask
    are probably designed for golfers' needs.

Nor let those clouds pretend that they are mountains.
    The wild moraine, the glacier, the peak
are, as you see, an accident of vision,
    a transient, though incandescent, freak.

And that's not music that surpasses Mozart
    with a more magical flute than aught he played with.
It is a flaw of the wind and two late blackbirds,
    or what the wind and the blackbird's song are made
        with.

And you're not young, as you suppose and wearing
    strange silks, nor with a lady at your side
that would have been a princess in Palmyra,
    walking beside her lover as a bride.

O no! she does not wear night for a mantle,
    nor is a star entangled in her tresses,
nor have you words in syllables of fire,
    flame by dark flame, to match dark lovelinesses.

Nor are you two beside that ancient river
    where, like ascending angels, the swans climb,
lovers together in the rose-communion
    of love the flower with her sister Time.

There is another way.   O lovely mirage,
    cheat of the heart, we know you what you are,
and still we follow, like the Kings before us,
    because it is impossible, the star.

GREEN LEMONS

Here are green lemons!
They scarcely move the leaves
where against the mountains
the dawn-scented eves
in the dark unspoken,
like ships in typhoon,
are lost for ever
under a moon
that sinks, and is crying
with voiceless white:
" All is foundered
in the night."
when God in pity
touches and changes
the stone-pale city
or the mountain-ranges
with the sour wonder
of the unripened fruit.
And the bright splendour
of a flute
untouched by fingers
shudders and falls
by the dark, the Trojan
the forsaken walls.
They scarcely move—the leaves.
But there is a far summons
from the mountains untrodden.
Here are green lemons.

I WROTE these poems more or less
out of the heart's bitterness.
But now they are written and over
I remember my London, my lover.
I was a young man, who am young no longer,
O love of my youth—shall the brown leaf wrong her?
There's a street that my feet cannot find or tread
where I went when I meant what I dreamed and I said,
London, when my star was as near and as far
as the dream and the things that we dream of are.
"Boy," you whispered, "O boy be kind
to your own poor heart, to your own bright mind,
in the days when the heart is dull, and duller
the mind as colour fades after colour.
And it will not matter to fail, but nail your
dream to the wooden cross of failure,
nails in the hands, nails in the feet,
and a Crucifix in Fitzroy Street."
I have nailed the dream and have turned away
the first day and the second day.
But the third day in my own hands and feet
shall I feel the nails in Fitzroy Street?

THE FIR TREE AND THE PALM

(*Adapted*)

A FIR-TREE in the Northland
  by Basel on the Rhine,
ensorcelled by the snowflakes
  dreams on the old inn-sign.

The air grows warm and fragrant
  with frankincense and balm,
and past her sister fir-trees
  she sees a single palm.

The bells that rock the steeple
  seem to her no such things,
but bright upon the mountain
  are mule-bells for the kings.

Beyond the Teuton voices
  with no familiar sound
she hears their starlit accent
  who walk together crowned.

She almost knows their meaning
  as though she made with them
the other Golden Journey
  that ends at Bethlehem.

But as they reach the village
  suddenly the magic breaks,
and at Basel in the Northland
  the trancèd fir-tree wakes.

And, while she cries on the palm-tree,
    she sees (returned from far)
on the sign The Three Kings painted,
    but over their heads the star.

CONVERSATIONS

CONVERSATION GALANTE

Surely it is not you.   Sit, nevertheless,
on the wicker-chair where a rag of your dress
was caught, and may, for all I know, be flying
a black signal-flag of the faith that we are denying.
So, sink back in the worn cushions! stretch your hand
with your dim gold air of a conductor, poising his wand
before the first bar of, " The Unfinished ".   Give the
    rail
the little decisive tap and then, powder-pale,
dim as dead music through lace, softer and dimmer,
let the notes out of smoke driftingly glimmer
into the first chord, that is the rag on the chair,
your outstretched hand, the sea-wrack of your hair
floating backwards on a cold ebb, and the light that dies
in those sconces that were, do you remember, your
    eyes!
So let us talk, though the affable phrases loiter
like news intercepted by an archangelic Reuter
of some vague ancient battle, some uneasy stir
between the unfallen ghosts of love and Lucifer.
" The days draw out."   " Really, this English weather."
(So we begin in social voices together.)
" Have you been well—that tiny patch on the lung? "
" Nothing! one can't, you know, be eternally young.
But you?   I hear so little these days.   Are you still
    writing? "
" What did I use to answer? "   " The swans are
    flighting."
" Well they have flown their last."   " But whither, and
    why? "
" After many summers (vide Tennyson) even swans
    die!
Slowlier they mount, crying, year after year until
the air over the lake is empty and the wings are still."
" And is there no echo in the heart of the vanished
    wings? "

" The sedge is withered on the lake and no bird sings."
" The Belle dame sans merci."   " When the heart beats
low we are all the knight-at-arms of Keats."
" And she—the sorceress? "   " Ah, she discovers
no trace in the dew of any last year's lovers.
Young and unchanging she moves in the teeth of time
safe in the long fidelities of rhyme,
queen of the instant, whose coronation is
the brief and brilliant anguish of the kiss."
" So bitter still! "   " If it be bitter to wonder
why the laurel trees are cut with the oleander,
why we walk no more in the woods, where note by note
song's falling fountain matched the blackbird's throat."
" And no way back? "   " The shades on Charon's bark
however they may entreat, are for the dark.
And had the gods, like Orpheus, tempted me,
you had not listened, nor followed, Eurydice."

" Then its good-bye again."   Ah, no! at most
the laying by another of a ghost
with the dim echo of a word, once said,
and now by both remembered, being dead.
" But I am keeping you.   And there's the bell! "
" No need to rise."   " And none to say ' Farewell '."

HOW A GIRL SAW IT

" FAME ?   I had forgotten fame—And yet
there must be something in it—For he let
all else go by in the wind—me and the wild
imagination of my unborn child—.
I was thinking of the child—what clear blue eyes
were cheated of the light, and what small wise
hands never fumbled at my breast.   The Abbey
with all its angels, puffing praise, grew shabby;
and the crying I never heard, and my poor pretty's
laughter made nonsense of the ' Nunc dimittis '.
Besides, what were they doing, all these great
ladies and gentlemen who sat in state
hearing the Bishop with a final air
give back to God what never started there.
And then the graveside—what sweet phantom crowder
played swifter than the priest's voice clearer, louder,
(like a child crying) ' O birth that failed of birth,
undusty dust, and earth that was not earth,
this is not death, but life unborn that flashes
here at the last ash out of alien ashes;
nor to the ground the dead departed brother
do we commit, but a mother that was no mother ! '

(There was a little cloud that drifted by
alone of all the legions of the sky—
bitter cold and white at first, until the sun
with unexpected benediction
laid roses in its heart.   So life might bless
with unanticipated tenderness
a fragile dream more exquisite, because
time cannot spoil the thing that never was.)

I took an hour of all his life and said
' Though all is dead, sweet hour, you are not dead.
I was a fool no doubt, but love's a school
where in her hour is wise and beautiful
even a girl such as I was, when he
of all his hours gave this one hour to me.
Love knows no difference, love has no degree,
in love the lovers are not bond nor free.
There is no king in love, there is no slave,
but what we take we lose, and what we give we have.
And I gave more, oh how much more! who could
give a whole life's unstartled maidenhood—

But if I hoard you, hour, I'll grow poor
who was so rich in giving, and so sure
of this my garnered wealth, and the small ghost
of my dream-child will be for ever lost
because I give no longer.   He passed by
my love and me, but if I let him lie
uncompanied in death by what I have
not he, but I, will wither in the grave.'

The others left him sleeping with his fame,
but I came back, that very night I came,
and where the pile of splendid wreaths was laid
set down my cloud, my hour of love, and said
' All that you had is yours to have no more—
fame will not comfort you on that cold floor
where windless airs beat in the broken frame—
there is no medicine for death in fame.
And all your other lovers have their term
even before the slow incessant worm.
They will not help, but I have found the way
of cheating the rigour of the grave.   I lay
my hour down and what I did not have
is sweet and actual within the grave.

128

My lonely cloud grows beautiful.   The sun
touches her with renunciation,
and there is born, unmortal, undefiled
by time or life, to you and me our child.' "

PUT in plain prose the thing's ridiculous,
A man like me, an old Solicitor
with a fair practice in conveyancing
and family business, should be sensible
even in dreams.   There goes a motor-bus
and that's a newsboy shouting in the Strand!
And yet there is a tree in the Temple Gardens
I watch the sun on.   You would be surprised
what birds it harbours, and how clear they sing,
as though the only law a bird and man
need know are just that trick of the lifted throat,
and the tossed radiance of a sound.

                                   The child
somehow got past my clerk, was in the room
before I noticed her.   First thing I knew
was a sense in the room of singing—a child's hair
moved by the wind is very like a song,
up, up in the light, and into shadows dipping,
and having secret access to the heart.
Besides a weak and wandering autumn sun
fell on her hair, and all those fallen leaves,
that step upon the ground with the sweet slur
of a child's stammer, when the words won't wait,
but blow on small and busy winds of thought—
those fallen leaves, I say, came in with her,
and with the leaves the lost October wood.

If I had had a child, she would have been
born in October; first thing she'd have watched
would have been the dancing leaves, and I'd have taken
one tiny hand, uncrumpled it to lay
a leaf inside it, so that, afterwards,
when she could walk, by virtue of the leaf

and of her childhood, we should find together,
just where the bracken ends, a young man waiting
beneath a birch—a solitary birch;
and presently a girl would come to him,
and these two would not kiss, but steadily
look on each other, and love would be born
instead of dying in October.   Then
these two would pass, but, where had been one birch,
they would be deep and quiet in a wood.

The seventh of October was the day
on which beneath the birch the young man waited
a long time since, and while he laughed, and waited
his lady had passed out into the wood,
that only the dead and children know.   My child
(if I had had one) had been born that day,
and might, I think, have led me to the wood.

Dreaming of course—but later, when I woke,
there was a leaf on the floor, and something else—
a bow that might have fastened a child's hair.

THE GAME

LET me remember, if I can.   High up
where the isle of Elba looks to Vastarös
through pine-trees, as a girl looks through her hair.
I waited for the Northern night.   The lake
mirrored no stars, for sky was a pearl-grey cloak
flung from the gleaming shoulder of a god
still in its curve true to the noble line,
and in its colour at his perfection hinting.
If steel were made with velvet then the pines
mirrored in the water were velvet, for so sharp
their outline, so unruffled but how soft!
Till there was a sigh too light to be the wind
too loud to be the murmur of the sea,
and yet an echo of that voice which, changing
from the full-throated gongs of wave on wave,
whispers along the archipelago
—the shadow of great trumpets—fainter falling,
till at the end on quiet Möleren
the voice is nothing but a sigh of the mist.
Thus Vastarös was hidden, thus the sky
the lake and even the wood in which I waited
were folded in the mist.   And there was a hush
as of an unseen crowd with bated breath
watching in some vast Roman amphitheatre
a game of life and death: but those who played
played not with steel and net, unless the wild
hair of a flying girl in the mist be a net
more fatal than the blade of a boy's love.
There was a shadow—light: a ghostly moon
or what was like the moon moved through the mist
with audible light creamily colouring
what else was cotton-white.   What would have been
on earth the horn of a coach over the hill
rose with no wheels, grew distant and was quiet.
Then the first player slipped between the wraiths,
herself, it seemed, as liable to the wind

as the warm clotted air she thus divided
with beauty so flashing that its brilliance hovered
like a substantial flame when mist returned.
Horn—music again—but O! how gold a horn
set to what lips, whose red was deeper guessed
than a red flower and like a flower slight
with mist and in that elfin moon.   So called
the second player, like discobolus,
reached one slim arm above his gracious head,
and, statue-perfect, leaning a little forward
as in the act to throw looked after her
in the immortal gesture of pursuit.
And in his turn the white mist covered him.

GOD AND THE DEVIL

God said to the devil
" I am tired, am tired of evil."

The devil replied as he would,
" and I am tired of good ! "

" Is there no end to evil ? "
God said (and He sighed) to the devil.

The devil replied, " T'will end
with goodness and you, my friend."

JESUS AND HIS FRIENDS

THE child Jesus went out seeking on His way
for a child like Himself in Bethlehem.
The dark-eyed children called Him to join their play,
but it was not in His spirit to play with them.

He had heavy thoughts in His mind of a child
borne down by their weight, and His heart was weary
for another boy who nor played nor smiled,
but walked alone with a world to carry.

Mary His mother had packed His load
with a little fruit and a cruse of wine,
and " Go not too far," said she, " on the road,
for the road Thou treadest is also mine."

The voice of the children playing, faded,
and Jesus, as always in solitude,
ran to the shade of the trees as they did,
but when He entered it was not their wood.

For the trees stood up like tall priests together,
and the scent of the flowers breathed upwards in myrrh,
and the small light feet through the moss and the
        heather
than the beat of His heart were quieter.

" Where is the friend of My soul," the child asked them,
" O bird, O blossom, O pine-tree, O feather? "
But, as though mere wonder had cloaked and masked
        them,
they shrank like a crowd of mourners together.

" Where is My friend ? " asked the grave child, seeking,
" with the spirit laden and the heart like Mine ? "
" Where is My friend ? " and, musingly, speaking
He broke the pomegranate and poured the wine.

The sap of the fruit ran down untasted.
" But My friend would both eat and understand,
and the wine of My mother had not been wasted,
nor had stained Me the palm of either hand."

" Where is My friend ? " and the wine dreeped, soaking
through the thirsty soil, and the broken fruit
lay among the grasses sullenly stroking
a small red mark, as He passed, on each foot.

" Where is My friend ? " and He went back tearless
to His mother's house, having found no friend,
the quiet Jesus, the gentle, the peerless,
alone as a child, and alone to the end.

KING AND CAT

SAID the King to the Cat
" What are you looking at? "

" At a mouse shivering
on your throne, O king
       That
is what I am looking at,"
     said the cat.

" Where is the mouse, O cat,
that you are looking at? "

" Do you not feel, O king,
Small, grey and shivering
       what
I am hunting at? "
     said the cat.

" Why draw so near me, that
I feel your cold breath, cat? "

" When the time has come to spring,
death—the old mouser—king
       doth
strike with his icy breath.
     Thus——" the cat saith.

PAVANE

S'DEATH if you must walk with him
I'll find a way to talk with him.
(Right and left, and so cross over!
and a cold partner for your lover!)

Custom of the dance?   So! faster!
An he need a dancing-master
I'll provide one, never fear me!
Nay! you need not cling so near me!

We'll tread a measure on green sward,
and for musicianer the sword
shall play's a tune will ravish one
or other with its motion.

Tears!   But late fountains at their task
of cooling the air of the heart.   Your mask
is loose.   I'll draw the strings.   You can
finish, close-masked, the high Pavane.

THE CARD-PARTY

LADY Millicent said with a purr
" My dear, what *can* he see in her? "
Mrs. Flip shrugged behind the tea-things,
" The duller they are, the more men see things."
" For me," said Lord Hen, " I like 'em bigger—
a girl's no good if she's got no figure."
The cavalry subaltern clicked his heels,
" A girl," he said, " is as good as she feels."
Lord Hen guffawed, " The damn young rip!
Eh, Millicent?   What, Mrs. Flip! "
Flip shifted her pince-nez on its ridge,
and said, " No doubt!—I'll ring for bridge."
The subaltern shuffled, " O, as you were; "
but this is what someone saw in her.

I   *Absence*

The pale room, like a swan
sailed down the even clear
stream of her absence, and a willow-tree
plunged in the glassy flow her pictured leaves
silver and silent and diaphanous.
Flawless the ripples circled round the reeds,
in their cold corridors no fishes swayed,
and no sweet breathing kine, from clover stepping,
broke up the level brushwork of the sun—
and the swan drifted, drifted in a dream.

" I suppose," the subaltern said, as he dealt,
" she's plenty of what the Bosche calls, ' gelt '?"
" None!   And two hearts," said Flip.   " That's rummy!
Three hearts," said Hen.   " Will you *look* at Dummy."
" That's game to you," murmured Millicent,
" I thought he'd forgotten her when she went."

" Not he," said Lord Hen, " the cheerful ass—
keener than ever it seems.   I pass."
" She paints, they tell me, one of the Slade's
beauties," said Millicent, " They went spades! "
" And he writes verse.   No wonder they click."
Said the cavalry subaltern, " that's our trick."
" The truth I expect, if you only know it,"
said Flip, " is she tells him he's a poet."

And Flip as it happened was on the track
of what the lad felt when he got her back.

II   *Return*

When she came back
the room unfolding her great wings
—white eagle of the water—left the stream
that woke into its murmurous daily life
of frothless-breaking ripples in clear foam,
of dragon-flies tatting the stretchéd air
with sudden criss-cross patterns of wild blue,
of half-seen trout that, glimmering as they oar,
look cooler than the cool in which they float,
of the wind stammering among the reeds,
" Syrinx " in soft and broken sentences,
She left the murmurous stream, and, without cry,
straight upward like a falling plummet fell
into the cold, the imperceptible quiet
where the great birds of music poise their wings.

" Well done, partner," chuckled the sub.
" Hearts were the ticket.   That's our rub."
" Perhaps," said Flip, " to save future trouble,
you'll say what in heaven made you double."
" Well," said his lordship, " What if I did? "

" I always double when hearts are bid."
" What does he mean," asked Flip.   " Perhaps,
I'm one of those tender-hearted chaps,"
said Hen, " who sympathize in starts
with fools, like those, who call high in hearts."
" Only his joke," said her ladyship,
" Dear at a fiver," rapped out Flip.

THE shapes we fashioned
   as I guess
reproach their own
   unworthiness,

saying: " Master, who
   made us, where
is Gabriel's trumpet,
   the fallen hair

about her shoulders
   of Rapunzel,
and the flute of Orpheus
   lost in Hell? "

We bend before them,
   and answer: " Wait!
Lovely, impatient,
   regenerate.

No breath of ours
   can wind the still
gold trumpet like
   a daffodil

heavy in heaven
   with the scent
of Time's unpromised
   increment.

Nor ours as we choose
   to climb
by golden tresses
   out of time,

nor down the falling floors
   to follow
Orpheus conniving with
   Apollo."

Not ours! but wait,
   twixt sleep and waking,
not by our will,
   nor of our making,

but in despite of what
   we sought,
unsummoned, uncontrolled,
   unthought,

to lips beyond the
   world is laid
the trumpet, golden
   braid by braid

the falling hair, and
   absolute,
not by our fingers
   touched, the flute.

THE ANSWER

WHAT do you answer, heart, when pain
        comes again?
I beat.   I have no other art,
        says heart.

Mind, is there any way of meeting
        the heart's beating?
There is no way that I can find,
        says mind.

And when these two have lost control,
        what follows, soul?
Three in one, and one in three,
        says she.

Then God, who hast deserted me
        on the black tree
again, what answer?   Thomas, I
        am the reply.

THE PIER-GLASS

K

THE PLANT AS

THE PIER-GLASS

THERE was no sigh when the pier-glass was broken.
She had lifted her hand slowly without thought,
as though to lift her hand were not a miracle,
as though the blood had not triumphed in terrible
    battles,
so that the slender arm might be curved upon the air,
and the fingers might touch the dark hair lightly,
as they used to do.

Or there had been a bowl of flowers set on a table,
a Dutchman's garland of terra-cotta against bamboo-
    green,
unconstrained, quiet, but not breathing perfume.
For the mirror reflected only the bare bones of beauty,
and the skull is fairer than the flesh that veils it,
for the attribute of loveliness is skin-deep, but the
    essence
is in the form of the bone.

Or it was an empty room, and the sun knocking
with golden double raps at the window—bright post-
    man
delivering letters that need never be opened—,
because the mirror easily read the celestial message
of the brilliant oblongs chess-patterned on the floor,
till dusk—the dark housemaid—came with her besom,
and swept them to limbo.

But now she does not lift her hand to her hair,
for the miracle is over and blood has lost the battle,
nor do the Dutch flowers glimmer in the bowl of brass,

147

and though the sun still raps at the window,
the dust scribbles across the scattered letters,
" Gone away.   Address unknown ! "
And the pier-glass is broken.

THE APPLE TREES

THE apple-trees were everywhere in blossom,
but the young men hacked at the trunks with axes
so that they might not be disturbed by the flower,
now or ever again when spring renewed its urgent
  message.
Slowly the petals drifted to the ground,
and presently the young grass was gay with a world of
  bloom,
as though a celestial garden had fallen from heaven,
as though a heavenly gardener had come overnight,
and bedded out the borders with a vision of the walls
rose-coral, and pink jacinth and a far hint of the lapis.
I wish that the young men had left the blossom unrifled,
I wish that in another spring there would be a new
  splendour
of rose-coral, pink jacinth and the unsurmountable
  lapis.
But they have gone into the further wood with their
  axes,
and I am alone with the fallen blossom and the ruined
  trees.
I cannot save you, flowers, I cannot help you, trees,
but here I have taken one blossom of all your blossoms,
where no steel can trouble and no ambition destroy.
Bloom, apple-blossom, on my grave and their grave.

HARES

I THINK that men who would hunt hares
would hunt anything.
I had a dream that made her form
on the green side of a mountain.
Swift were the feet of my dream.
Sportsmen, hunting a hare in the valley,
lost her, and the straying hounds put up my dream.
" Hounds are mad," said the huntsmen, calling them
off.
" Let them be," said the master, crashing through
gentians,
" There is no prettier sport than a mountain-hare.
Find her, hounds, find her, find her ! "
But the hounds lost her scent among flowers,
and returned, dragging their tired bodies at nightfall.
For the hounds of the valley will never catch the
mountain-hare,
as long as her scent is one with the scent of the flowers.
But some day they will try again,
for men, who will hunt hares,
will hunt anything.

MUSIC IN SILENCE

THERE is also music in silence—
those three tall women, of whom I have read,
they do not play the harp or the viol.
They let the thread trawl through their fingers,
till one, leaning forward, sunders it
with scissors that were dipped, I think, in the moon.
Is it nothing that the leopard in the brake
moves quieter than the rustle of the grasses?
Is it nothing that the shadow of a bird's wing
may hover like a cloud on a cornfield,
a cloud no bigger than a bird's wing?
the roots of the flower in the silent earth,
the unborn child in the womb,
and the unguessed thought in the poet's mind—
these are three marvels, yea, I know none greater—
there is also music in silence.

EIGHT SONNETS

DEDICATION

Honour (if there be honour) where honour is due!
   I have written as I could.   I have no fear
of judgment if I failed.   For this I knew
   that, if a man be deaf, he can only hear
imagined sounds, fainter than real and few,
   and if a man, being blind, is called to steer
his beacons will be lights that memory drew
   out of the past, aching to disappear.
But even were they marshlights I pursued,
   and all I heard a transitory clef,
   I walked the path not chosen but assigned.
You made no stranger of my solitude,
   you heard especially when I was deaf,
   and saw in my behalf when I was blind.

DON QUIXOTE

Don Quixote de la Mancha, the last knight,
   scrapes rusty blade along the sheath all rust,
dons creaking mail that will not settle right,
   nor sees the crooked helm how dark with dust.
The crazy vizor dims his crazier sight,
   his mailèd hands hang like a piece of crust,
and Rosinante steams as though she might
   have drenched herself with wine that turned to must.

Slowly he rides, the perfect mark of laughter,
   in search of what Childe Rolande never had,
   of what King Arthur dreamed to, and forgot.
Yet all the secret soul of man rides after,
   whose heart is all they know of Galahad
   whose knighthood all they have of Lancelot.

Jesus was a flockmaster. And George Moore drew
    Him
  lifted from the Cross by Joseph, back again
among the mountainy yowes and lambs that knew
    Him
  as their beloved Shepherd. He was fain
if men refused to find salvation through Him,
  (the tale continues) to bid the wind and rain,
and the long silence as Saviour to renew Him,
  once of the world, now of a mountain pen.
Nor is there need to challenge or reprove
  George Moore for having drawn Him as a hind.
  When faith and hope are self-destructive shams
when charity has everything but love,
  when all we ask of vision is to blind,
  Jesus in spring is safer with the lambs.

THIS NIGHT

And not in vain this midnight has been numbered
   among the myriad nights, nor did it fade
vainly into the lost, the unremembered
   darkness of which this bubble earth is made.
Some were awakened to beauty, who had slumbered;
   some found the courage of pain, who were afraid;
some watched through dormer windows unen-
    cumbered
   love, like the moon, ride high and one man prayed:
" Carry me outwards on your flood, cool night,
   on your cowled wave into your cloistered deep
   with not a sound nor movement, save the dim
last carillon that tolls for the last light,
   as the sun sets for ever into sleep,
   and God, made in his image, sets with him."

URSULINE

NOT with thy pain, but with mine known and scorned,
   O delicately fair! take thou thy place
among those women that beauty has suborned
   by mere excess of her prevailing grace.
Perilous as autumn woods with death adorned
   and the red leaf, deciduous in embrace
let thy new lover by thy first be warned
   that those are snowbound lilies in thy face.
And what will thaw discover but the low drop
   of curtained eyelids over eyes half-seen,
or in the whiter breast than the first snowdrop
   the pale refusal of an Ursuline?
O April thou and winter! wilt thou cozen
this fool until he freeze, as I am frozen?

QUIET

So quiet that the crystal feet of the rain
   gliding from blade to blade were almost heard,
so quiet that the small invisible grain
   within the corn-husk whispered when it stirred,
so quiet that the trees across the plain
   trembled through all their branches when one bird
suddenly cried, and then was still again,
   as though he also to the spell deferred.
Those who, they knew not now, had hither strayed,
   wondered, half doubted, wavered, last enthralled
   into the stillness passed with arms outspread.
There was no reason they should be afraid,
   nor need to ask what name the place was called.
   They did not know, nor care, if they were dead.

UNPLUCKED, A MOUNTAIN-LILY

IF after all these gentle years it seem
   that I am moody and bewildered, pardon
a man self-banished in the idle dream
   of paths he knew in a forgotten garden.
He walks between the darkness and a gleam
   where once bloomed flowers no earthly fragrance
      stirred on,
and where beside a visionary stream
   he for a moment laid aside his burden.
So might an alpine shepherd in September,
   as the ice closed the passes slowly follow
      the sound of bells descending to the valley,
and, as he left the peaks of spring, remember
   that when he had climbed at the challenge of the
      swallow
   he had found, and left unplucked, a mountain-lily.

THE LAST SONNET

Dark Lady, I have found your light at last
    unveiled, and at the last have turned my eyes
lest that fair future should destroy the past,
    and make an earth of what was Paradise.
Ah! you were lovely here, but now, being fled,
    your bodiless beauty by no passion trammelled
rises, not pale among the paler dead,
    but Indian treasure with the night enamelled.
But since your barren beauty thus can breed,
    itself transmuted by some seed that stirs
the mateless dead, turning to earth, I plead
    that, in the recollection of my verse,
the days we wasted and the love that tarried
in these two beauties may be matched and married.

WINTER

WINTER

I HAVE supposed that when the time shall be weary
    of turning the orb of earth in his strong fist,
he will lay it aside with his crown and sceptre,
    and there will be no dawn in the East, nor a twilit
      West.

He will drop his chin pensively on his crooked elbow,
    and the days will eddy about him like dead leaves,
but he will not heed their rustle or anything,
    when there is not noontide nor green-fading eves.

He will be thinking of the desire of godhead,
    and, though himself immortal, he will only know
that it is motionless and is as silent
    as a falling snowflake on the untrodden snow.

And he will understand that the spring and summer
    and the ripening sheaves are neither willed nor
    planned,
but were only the heat between his fingers
    as he turned the orb abandoned in his great hand.

And slowly the frost will trace its patterns,
    and bind him like Merlin with the creeping frond
of fretted ice, and the waving hands of snowflakes ;
    but he will look steadily to a light beyond

the dark light of the glacier, and the half-light
    of snow drifting and heaping when there is no sun,
and he will know that there is fulfilment
    when the orb in his hand is no longer spun.

165

Time and his world will be a part of winter—
    like the cold and glacial moon, as fair, as still—
and there will be no sound even of sighing,
    when God in Time unthroned accomplishes His will.

COUNTRYMAN'S WINTER

I

BEFORE the snow was trodden in Shipley Glen
   I have plunged deep between the tattered trees
as proud and lonely as great Nansen when
   he passed the ice-cliffs of the Polar Seas.
Like him I saw beyond the haunts of men
   Nature untroubled breathing at her ease,
and watched the snowflakes dip and rise again,
   brushing upon my lips like silver bees.
And at Dick Hudson's under Rombald's Moor
   farm-labourers like ploughmen in a book
gathered and drank their beer.   I am not sure
   if there were settles or an ingle-nook,
but this I know, they did not speak at all,
and stared indifferently at the wall.

II

Well! that was country winter.   Nothing odd
   to those who live with trees all year and know
what time the leaves will crumple, when the mud
   will smear the lanes, and what winds threaten snow,
but to a boy, who wearily has trod
   streets, where dull houses stretch in endless row,
strange as the music of the woodland god
   heard in soft lands where oleanders grow.
The idle boors speechlessly drank their ale,
   clattered their mugs, and dumbly separated,
but I who read their movements like a tale
   by Thomas Hardy in charmed silence waited.
Then with a happy sigh, but head bent down,
trudged back through moonlit snow to Bradford town.

WHEN God made Eden, I believe,
He had a garden up His sleeve
not meant for mother Eve and Adam,
but for their children when they had 'em.

Not with tall trees, and miles of sward
offering green incense to the Lord,
nor with great vistas set, like blue
windows that God is looking through.

But planned, although a private place
about the length a child can race,
as carefully as when He bent
the globe to make a continent.

A range of hills upon the West,
a miniature of Everest,
with three-inch pines, whose ranks advance
through microscopic gentians,

but leaning a little, as though they were
waiting to leap the glacier,
and wade knee-deep in argent rows,
the small, but everlasting snows.

And in the centre there would be
the dark, unharvestable sea,
drawing a Lilliputian tide
from yellow beaches twelve-foot wide,

yet wide enough for lads to slip
the lean enquiring pirate-ship,
that sails, with youth upon the beam,
the long adventure of the dream.

For in the North the ice-floes call
the small, precarious admiral
to wear beyond the sun, and find
a world, where all are stricken blind.

Where in a cold and grinding hush
the icy arms of danger crush
the little captain, and his bark—
and all, except his heart, is dark.

Or Southward, where the olive trees
hang on the tiny terraces
like puffs of smoke, and all day keep
the quiet attitudes of sleep,

and oleander to her mouth
draws all the summer in the South,
and in the night the fireflies
paint golden maps of Paradise.

Or in the jungle of the East
glitters some smooth, recurrent beast—
the tiger's stripe, the leopard's stars,
bright as the butt-end of cigars,

while with cold eyes that look beyond
embroidered arch and lily-pond,
from period to period
broods in his shrine the lotus-god.

This Eden inside Eden He
made for you, children, furtively,
and never told the Serpent, or
the Archangel, who guards the door.

And thus it was that Abel found
the sword swept four foot from the ground,
and wasn't meant (the thing was plain!)
to interfere with him and Cain.

So, while their parents delved and span
in the cold world outside, they ran
to Eden's gate, and just slipped through
beneath the sword—and so can you!

SOLDIER'S WINTER

ALPENGLOW
upon the Scottish hills, changing the snow
with one great brush-stroke to an arras woven
of the moss-roses from the sills of heaven.

And soon, how soon,
on swan-wings drifting down a slender moon
will watch—a heavenly Midas—in bright alarm
a world all silver in her silver arm.

So night to dawn
offers, defeated, his last sable pawn,
while she with the flushed gambit of the sun
sweeps the great board and mates his king in one.

Or when the mist
strangles the valleys with his naked fist
and the sorrow for all things wasted beneath the sky
is gathered in a single curlew's cry,

then, O then,
deep in the heart for all the mountain-men,
for all that broken jetsam of the war
the pipes play " Lochaber no more."

Spring is not spring, nor summer summer
when the snow-flake sorrows eddy and clamour,
cold as the stone in the farthest scaur,
and wild with " Lochaber no more,
Lochaber, Lochaber, Lochaber no more."

There is no sun now nor any moon,
but out of the mist a ghostly tune
not on the high and hunting air
of the Northern wind, but everywhere,
that love remembers and (clearer yet)
when the loves forgotten themselves forget!

" For the body no haven, the heart no harbour
and over the screaming tides of war
the pipes play Lochaber, the pipes play Lochaber,
the pipes play Lochaber, Lochaber no more."

REVELLER'S AND FIRESIDE WINTER

MADAM, it seems that Thames is frozen over.
  Could we not, donning vizors, leave the dance,
and with the stars for link-boys let a lover
  lead to the sheeted tideways of romance?

Let music be. Our souls will find a string
  when the vielle and dulcimer are mute,
fit for an angel softly fingering
  love's overture upon a treble-lute.

Aye, chairman, set us down. We're for a ball
  where neither sword nor patches are allowed,
but only the simple heart that, stripped of all
  but love, can dance lavoltas on a cloud.

We shall not need those shoes with wings of steel,
  like Mercury's, on which the Dutchmen skate
their wolds, who, if we lift our forehead, feel
  the air blown backward by the speed of Fate.

Beneath us, as we glide, becalmed the stream
  strains at the cables of the frost, but we,
who until this were anchored to a dream,
  may cast off now, and set the sails for sea.

THE POET'S WINTER

You shining company! there waits without
the quiet rooms of heaven in the snow
one who distraught by equal love and doubt
now seeks to enter, and now turns to go.

He has heard you speaking gently from afar,
and was drawn hither sweetly against his will,
but scarce can see the window for the star,
set like a lamp upon the window-sill.

Nor is it actual snow, though banked and driven
against your door that holds him from the latch,
but deeper drifts to music heaped in heaven
than foot can measure or than time dare snatch.

Yet though benighted, wandered, and in storm,
no need to bid him for an alms to enter,
who walks in the mere shadow of song as warm
as a lamb folded in a poet's winter.

GOD AND MARY'S WINTER

THIS leafless beech envies the fir
that needs not spring to burnish her,
but when the winter world is black
defies with green the almanac.

An eager wind upon the boughs,
empty as a deserted house,
knocks loudly, and then listens shocked
at the grim silence on which he knocked.

His startled footsteps ring so loud,
he does not hear the little crowd
of rustling guests behind the fence
between this world and that one dance.

He does not see, like coloured paper
moths veering round a phantom taper,
the leaves return to haunt the tree's
dark rooms and quiet passages.

He knocks again, remembering
the company she kept in spring.
Silence! He stamps, and, leaving her,
calls on the hospitable fir.

Now the wind goes. The cold air huddles
so close it seems to crush the needles,
while, violin to violins
whispering far, the snow begins.

And now those branches almost ache
under the fingers, flake by flake,
that chase their haggard outlines with
the pencils of a silversmith.

Each bough so whitens with the brittle
surface of newly hammered metal,
you'd think Cellini carved the tree
twig by twig in filigree.

The beech-tree, as the snowflakes cease,
falls with the fir upon the peace
that may have folded branch and stem
the olive-trees at Bethlehem.

EPILOGUE

SEPTEMBER, leaning backward, in that strange year
   looked in the eyes of summer and forgot
(or did not care) that so Queen Guinevere
       had walked with Lancelot.

Her minstrels of the Court, the thrush, the wren,
   and April's blackbird under autumn leaves
with rapture mad, or feigned, sang back again
       green dawns and golden eves,

as though the winter were an idle tale,
   and never leaves would fall nor throats be dumb,
nor ever the heart change, nor beauty fail,
       nor Arthur ever come,

as though in some immortal reckoning
   an instant of light outlasts an age of dark,
and death stood still to hear the thrushes sing—
       as these are singing.   Hark!

CHRISTMAS POEM

Iᴛ is winter in the mountain
  where the wind confesses the firs.
They have put on the veil, the green ones,
  the slender, the whisperers.

" I loved the sun, and I gave him
  all that he asked," said this.
" Is it sin? "   " It is sin," said the North wind,
  " to be ashamed of the kiss."

" I was taller than my sisters,"
  said that.   " Is it sin to be proud? "
" It is sin," said the wind, " to be lovely,
  and go with the fair head bowed."

" But the hare leaped over my branches,"
  said the smallest.   " Have I sinned? "
" Suffer the little fir-trees
  to come unto me," said the wind.

LIGHT THE CANDLES!

LIGHT the candles again! Let each clear flame
speak for the past—a hope, a vision, a doubt.
Let these return as ghosts who, when they came,
with their own breath blew their own dimness out,

and put on fire for an instant. Let them prove
that they are not vanquished, but are hoarded at most,
that in the long astonishment of love
death is the only irreparable ghost.

And even death has mercy in his season
when the needles of the fir, heaping upon his sandals
check him, and, with a bountiful brief treason
to his own darkness, he pauses. Light the candles!

LIKE voices whispering in a room deserted,
the flames of the dead fir-trees, delicate
avenues that taper into childhood, stain—
look, if you dare, ageing and heavy-hearted!—
the years that were so swift they would not wait,
all the swift years that will not come again.

Christmas! Put out the candles! Let the branches,
and all their needles, into darkness dwindle;
let mercy, as at dawn the lamplighter
snuffed the old street-lamps, quench those dazzling
        inches
flame upon flame, pale candle after candle!
Let night enfold them all—save the one fir

that the hare leaped in the forest. Let us go
into the woods and find it—green and young
before the axe and the accolade of fire.
We shall forget—and it need never know—
that hearts—and fir-trees—must be warped and wrung
by time, and life's impossible desire.

CHRISTMAS 1938

Now almost at the year's end
there comes the ancient lull
of a how perilous peace!
We have suffered. Let us pretend
that what was dark or dangerous or dull
shines on the king of the trees
as the candles shine bravely
with their doomed inch of clear light,
as the cries of children glitter.
Harshly the days have passed and gravely;
there was always, it seemed, a deeper night;
and after the bitter dawn a dawn more bitter.
Here is the pause. Here is the time to cherish
hope that stumbles out of the midnight storm.
Here we may love for an instant instead of hating.
Now the lights sink, and the tapers perish,
but we who were cold are suddenly warm.
What is the comer for whom we are waiting?
Who knows? Who guesses? The night is holy;
it grows so quiet you can almost hear
the heart-stroke held on a single beat—
it hangs so long, it moves so slowly.
Or is it in the darkness drawing near
across the centuries the sound of feet
drawing back, drawing over? Far, yes far
the feet have wandered: they were almost gone.
What bell has spoken we thought was dumb?
No need to answer: too late to bar
the door which the hand is laid upon.
Lost and benighted! the dawn has come!

WIRELESS

Now the heart has passed beyond
  her last interpreter
verse, the diaphanous bond
  wherewith speech fettered her.

Now the mind, like a flower printing
  its shape upon eyes blind,
is borne, with naught preventing,
  directly on the mind.

Now the soul has surrendered
  to a force it did not guess
the far stations sundered
  by spoken speechlessness,

keyed to a signal flung farther
  than the word's decadent spark,
whose brightness did but gather
  and point the deepening dark.

The great towers stand idle,
  but we at this Midnight are
swept into touch on the tidal
  wave-length of the Star.

THE DONKEY AND THE ARK

THE ARK

Noah he said to the kangaroo:
" I'm afraid that we haven't got room for you.
We contracted for birds, we contracted for fishes,
for the beasts wot run, and the snake wot swishes,
but, believe you me, I am going to stop
at a crazy brute that can only hop."

(There were Ham and Japhet as well as Shem.
I hope that you haven't forgotten them.)

And Mrs. Noah she upped and she said:
" Noah! it's time that the beasts was in bed.
Two million pillows, and twice that of sheet,
and one maid-of-all-work, my lad, it's a treat."
To which he replied: " Well! its less by two.
There won't be no bed for the kangaroo."

(Japhet looked down as meek as a lamb,
but privately signalled to Shem and to Ham.)

They pulled up the gangway they did, the crew,
and there on the quay sat the kangaroo.
But there wasn't no wind, and there wasn't no sea,
so he winked his eye—did that wallaby.
" There are three bright lads," says he, " in the Ark.
And I isn't afraid to go home in the dark."

(For Ham he had given his affidavit,
witnessed and sealed by Shem and by Japhet.)

So they poured out the drinks for father Noah,
till the bears looked like mice, and the mice protozoa;
and he chucked the elephants under the trunk,
and told the leopard his spots were drunk,
and he counted the lot, but he had to stop,
because one ran like a hare but two wouldn't hop.

(" And if two won't hop," says Noah to Shem
and Ham and Japhet, " I've done with them.")

So Noah he sat on the deck to curse
the absence of ready reckoners.
" Twice one is two, but I'm bothered," said he,
" if two don't sit and cock snooks at three.
I've asked, and I've begged till I'm fit to drop,
but never a wriggle, and never a hop."

(And I don't suppose that he murmured d——n,
nor neither does Japhet, nor Shem nor Ham.)

But they made a sign and with one great flop
Kangaroo leaped from the shore at the hop.
Noah he sees him and lets out a roar,
" Two short legs and two long 'uns make four."
And he turned round threatening-like on two
till he started to hop like the kangaroo.

(And that is the story, if you will belave it
of Kangaroo, Shem and Ham, and Japhet.)

IF I had a donkey who would not go
I would lay the stars at his angry toe.
I would whisper the music of the spheres
into his backward obstinate ears.
I would make him a halter twice as long
as the first clear note of the sirens' song.
I would pillage Olympus to get him hay
sweeter than ambrosia.
And, if at the end he was sulking still,
I would call up the ghost of English Will,
and purge his distempers and humours (God rot 'em)
by changing him back into Nicholas Bottom.

TURN AGAIN DICK WHITTINGTON

(See Note)

(Theme with Variations : A Contribution to Modern Technology.)

TURN again, Dick Whittington, turn!
That old rogue Samuel Wilkes
established the freedom of the Press,
so that the world might learn
what lies behind the withered silks
of nothingness.
Valiantly the spectres gibber,
poor rats behind the arras—
Polonii clenching the stuff in
dead men's teeth—but they only embarrass
the dignity of Styx—the oldest man ribber
that keeps on rollin' for ever and says nuffin'.
Because there is nuffin' to say?
Or because there is too much to impart
when death, with the vulture on his wrist,
lets fly at the Prometheus heart,
and the news of the day
is the blood of the journalist.
As the blood of Viscount Rothermere
is the seed of the Press.   Why else
should Dick Whittington turn?
Listen to Bow bells,
Beau Brummel bells and all's clear!
See how they burn!
They all ran after D. H. Lawrence,
but the curtain was clenched in the dead man's teeth,
so in a trice
walking like Dante beneath
the Ponte Vecchio in Florence
he cut off the tails of the mice.
Tailless mice at Arras or
tailless mice on the Somme,

where are you now beside the Shalimar?
Lord! let your kingdom come,
because there is none other that fightest for
the tailless mice that we are.
Where is Miölner?   Where is
the hammer of Hitler?   Where
is Cagliostro?
Where is Tinkerbell—O mère
Siegel of the fairies
ora pro nostro
Barrie et pro E. E. Cummings
and for the Transatlantic soul that bilks
the merciless chauffeur of tradition's car.
(Courtesy of Samuel Wilkes
you may hear the strummings
broadcast from Eliotsville, Pa.)
(Courtesy of Samuel Wilkes
Samuel Weller, allee same Uncle Sam.)
Argos the peacock unfolds
the lustige witwe melodrame
in fallen flowered silks
where the wind scolds
the ruffled feathery eyes,
and ah Gus! (vide George Robey and Stephen Leacock)
he shakes, he revolts.
Now the immortal peacock
suddenly cries
and moults.
La moult desirée—the forest lovers
all's one and very like a weasel
or backed like a whale.   Dick Whittington
turn round the picture on the easel,
lest somebody discovers
what really has been done.
And thou the younger Plato or Meleager
(or a chorus-ending from Euripides)
the broken bell rings out and is done.
There shall be no more seas.

Aye, Lady Macbeth, it is a dagger.
Turn, for the last time turn, Dick Whittington.

Note.—For the better comprehension of this poem readers are recommended to begin by mastering all the volumes in the British Museum. A knowledge of Middle Aramaic, though not indispensable, will be helpful.

VALEDICTORY

INTERNATIONAL LABOUR OFFICE

ALBERT THOMAS, Director of the I.L.O.,
and Arthur Fontaine, Chairman of the Governing
    Board,
have wagged their beards for the last time.
At Petit Saconnex
the old Office is a modern Hotel,
and in the Route de Lausanne
a new and beardless Director
looks out vaguely at the lake,
wondering at his chubby King Hal ease
if his game of tennis will be interrupted by the Bise.

Dans cette nuit immense
Qu'allez vous faire si loin d'ici,
Albert et Arthur?   La parole est à vous.
There is no second International in death,
Albert, but only the first international
of the white-moth dead, who form no groups,
pass no Conventions, do not tear their beards,
nor with a sudden flight of the eagle tower,
where only the heart of the bird in silence speaks
to the snow-silence of the mountain-peaks.

And, Arthur, Rhadamanthus makes
no special exemptions for the French,
even for one who with delicate swift gestures
can make all judgment seem ridiculous,
save a summing-up in favour of l'esprit Gaulois.
And the gold colour of Monet, and the misty palette
of Carrière are scattered, and your mild eyes
must look where unknown painters mix
their midnight water-colours by the Styx.

Flush at evening on Mont Blanc seen from the Board-
    room,
sound of the cattle-bells in the steep lane outside the
    garden,
or the snow beating against the window of the Hotel
    Belle-vue,
or against the high balcony in the Rue Mont Blanc,
or the mouettes cutting a sword path with the moon
    to Belle-Rive,
and the Jura guarding the peace of Genève for all the
    world,
never again, Albert, never again, Arthur, but instead
memory while any of us can still remember
of two bons bourgeois, who on the point of a lance
carried the pennant of triumphant France.

ARNOLD BENNETT

Now that Arnold Bennett whom we cherished is dead,
    and Robert Bridges, that inveterate deep lover
of life will not toss again his lion head,
    it is time to look back and tell their virtues over.
There was always a space, Arnold, in what you said,
    a pretended stammer of thought as though to cover
the young, and in spite of life the astonishèd
    fancies that cried as sadly as the wheeling plover
over the empty autumn fields to the spring.   " Return!
    Where are your snowdrops now that the bracken's
        brown?
    Is there not always spring in a bird's sight? "
You also, Arnold, in the autumn would not learn
    that the lilies crumple and the cowslips are trodden
        down.
     " Come back! " you were always crying, and you
     were right.

AND you, Robert Bridges, you made your last will
  and testament of beauty in the winter of your
    thought,
but there was no snow of the mind falling upon Boar's
    Hill,
  nor upon the further fields that your vision sought.
You could have lingered a year with a daffodil,
  pondering on the dust that could be so brightly
    fraught
with unaccountable design, and yet could find the
    thrill
  of all matter for ever prevailing upon nought.
Long were your years, but their orbit was inwards
  to the quiet at the heart of the cyclone where leaves
  and the butterflies hang as still as in amber,
or as dew on the crocus before it draws sunwards.
  You are flown, you are melted but, when no wind
    grieves,
    in the calm of the evening we shall remember.

DARK RIOUPÉROUX

IT was raining, Flecker, in dark Rioupéroux.
  All Grésivaudan's vale was hidden with cloud.
But, as I passed beside the river, you
  stood at my shoulder, as though the mist allowed
your gentle ghost to walk. "It is not true,
  (or is it true?)" you murmured, "that when I vowed
that I'd return to tramp the valley through
  like any other boy among the crowd,
that this return was meant. For when I speak
  none answers: if I stretch my hands, none knows.
I am become as distant as the peak
  and colder than the quiet on the snows."
Still so impatient! But in Rioupéroux
who looks for love and youth finds only you.

I DROVE OUT FROM GRENOBLE IN THE BUS

I DROVE out from Grenoble in the bus,
   rocked with the sun that poured in bushels of wheat
his midday harvest over all of us,
   so that we paddled gold.   Is it not sweet,
not fine, I mused, to be a king, and thus
   to ride in triumph through the conquered street
of youth's Persepolis?   Aye marvellous
   merely by riding to retrieve defeat.
What then?   Have you no answer, poet, you
   that were so eloquent in the rain falling?
   Can death be jealous of my life's reveilles?
Here are the mountains, here Rioupéroux,
   and here a voice you knew at Oxford calling.
   " Almost my feet were gone.   Return, Techelles."

G. K. CHESTERTON

Now let the trumpets of the sunlight spatter
   the routed thunder rolling with the drums,
and let the enemies of darkness scatter.
   Let the great gate swing open. A hero comes.

Like John of Austria from conquest riding
   doubting himself, when nothing else dared doubt
     him,
he climbs, unconscious of the glory chiding
   the tattered cloak of wit he wraps about him.

When all was still, save for the evil pealing
   of crooked chimes that on the midnight slurred
the raven musics of the Satyrs reeling
   out of the pit, his cap and bells were heard.

Like a great wind, after a night of thunder
   he rocked the sodden marshes of the soul,
and ripped the mists of cowardice asunder
   with laughter vivid as an aureole.

He does not need to knock against the gate,
   whose every action like a prayer ascended,
and beat upon the panels. Trumpets, wait
   for a hushed instant! We loved him. It is ended.

Do you remember the Trocadero, Drum,
   and the alcove where we dined by the wall?
I dined there again this evening,
   but you did not come at all.

Young men came in together, Drum,
   and looked wise and grand with their food.
They talked carelessly of to-morrow,
   as we did when we could.

They squandered the lovely moments, Drum,
   without fear or regret or doubt.
They had all the future before them,
   that we must be without.

They did not take each other's hand, Drum,
   for fear of loss, or death, or an end,
while the elderly man at the next table
   waited (they guessed) for his friend.

Strange how things never alter, Drum,
   and strange how they're never the same.
I sat in the alcove and waited,
   as I used, but you never came.

W. H. LOWE-WATSON

ALTHOUGH the dear and first-invited guest
   of life you would not stay, because you heard
voices inaudible to all the rest
   bidding you to some party you preferred

of your bright equals.   Yet we needs must rate
   their just impatience, seeing, that while we
had few and how brief hours they would not wait
   a little for your timeless company.

Go then, since they have summoned you, and go
   proudly by right, and as by habit gaily.
But, as you enter with your laurels, know
   that Love himself cries, " In aeternum vale."

RIOUPÉROUX RE-VISITED

It was before Elkin Matthews published " The Bridge
   of Fire "
   that we talked in your rooms beside the river,
   Flecker,
      in Oxford, when you were writing " Rioupéroux."
There was white Curaçoa on the table, ink and bent
   wire,
      an etching (first state) of Heidelberg and the Neckar
      crumpled but worth (you asserted) a pound or two.

And realms of paper for unwritten masterpieces,
   and eager pencils, most of them with the points
      broken,
      and books from Blackwell's, notably Ramal
      (Walter)
" When slim Miranda " as the dark increases,
   I hear you speak it again, as it was spoken
      with the slow husky drawl that the years cannot
      alter.

You thought that Masefield had some slight distasteful
      power,
   that Phillips was a charlatan, but felt that Yeats
   might, if he studied Baudelaire, still count.
" It is my faith," you cried, " that one black flower
   dropped from the Frenchman's hand will outperfume
      the Fates,
      and with dark glory rekindle the pale Pierian fount.

I will walk," you murmured, " in Grésivaudan's vale.
   I will see the mountains that brood above the river,
      whose snow-filled flood is like the soul of France—

cold as the ice it draws from, but with its current flail
    smashing the tangled undergrowth of lies that shiver
       at the swift terror in the waters of Romance.

Flow out of the mountains into the stolid plain,
    out of the hills of song into the lowlands of prose!
       That is your mission, and mine," you chanted,
         " Land
of the trouvère, of youth, of wine, of the stain
    of blood spilt at the barricades—the rose,
       whose bitter scent the gods of freedom planned.

Yes, I will go to France again and tramp the valley
       through."
    Meanwhile the great laburnum with its golden bees
       swarming in the green hive glimmered in the quiet
       Cher,
and the evening gathered and deepened before we knew
    that the dark was upon us, and the silences,
       where each dim blossom matched and marked a
       star.

" Before we knew that the dark was upon us."   Yester-
    day,
    after the thousand years of which you wrote, I stood
       under the rain beside the river, and the mill.
I have forgotten what it is ghosts say,
    or by what signal a stricken spirit could
       win back to speech from the dark where all is still.

I heard your dangerous dim voice, so sweet
    that had I answered, and made my voice to carry
       beyond the slow forgetful flood in the hush,
it would have sewn the crocus at your feet
    among the asphodel, and where no song-birds tarry
       have starred the dome of Hell with the notes of the
       thrush.

I did not speak, Flecker, I could only linger
   with helpless hands outstretched in a midsummer
     cold as the darkest of December eves.
But as I stood, I heard a later singer
   speak for us both, and thought, " Salute, new-
     comer,"
   and heard an echo through a world of leaves.

GERALD GOULD

Gerald, I remember to-day, and perhaps you re-
    member
an autumn evening when we sat by the fire,
(fifteen years ago it was, and we were not old then),
and spoke, as the bitter wind outside shouted " No-
    vember ",
of the poet's aching mission and the heart's desire,
and all the secrets of life that were untold then.

You with that strange fair look of a cherub caught
in a net of stars and the laws of Smith and Jevons,
urged as you always did the cause of Labour.
But as I watched your eyes under your greying hair,
    I thought,
" Here is a creature, lost out of what incredible heavens,
rewriting political economy with lute and tabor."

" But what does that matter," I thought, " he is of the
    movers
and makers of the world by the strength of his dream.
Fools act and babble, but the dream in the end pre-
    vails."
Yes, Gerald, but before you had satisfied your lovers,
before the rill in the mountains had widened into the
    stream,
you left us to find the other nightingales

whose song has troubled the quiet upland pasture
of Tempe.   You are walking with your own
and they are glad.   But we for whom your song
broke, as across the edge of hope you cast your
lariat of dreams, are beggared and alone;
and the days that you made short, Gerald, are long.

Hail and farewell, you dearest head, farewell!
And take with you wherever your foot strays
with the old careless sweetness of despair
this flower of verse, whose small and earthly smell
is but the shadow of the unearthly bays
the Muse herself has laid upon your hair.

FOR OMAR

WHEN dawn no longer, with the hunters use,
    for you flung a bright noose,
and darkness in its everlasting net
    trapped dome and minaret,
was there a voice upon the further side
    in some dim tavern cried:
" All you, whose landlord is the Lord of Hosts,
    fill up your glasses, ghosts,
and, as you drain the shadow-bumper, feel
    how through veins stricken steal
the summer-heats that are the gift of verse
    and its great vintagers."
It is all over—life and love and song,
    you thought, and you were wrong!
For as the door flings open, the grey mist
    breaks for the lutanist!
Yes! from high-piping Pehlevi the rose
    about his footing grows,
and through his garden to the moon ascending,
    world without ending,
in Hell and over silence shall prevail
    the Persian nightingale.
Ghosts to your feet! No heel-taps, drink and cry
    " Mud in the devil's eye! "
When song and wine and Omar to their Hell come,
the place is heaven and the password, " Welcome! "

SIR ARTHUR STEEL-MAITLAND

BEYOND the failure that man calls success
are the difficult laurels for those whose word is " no ",
when easier men and smaller answer " yes ".
Into your peace, crowned with those laurels, go!

ARISTIDE BRIAND

THE Cyrano of Peace to those hereafter
  worthy to follow him doth here remit
the rapier of his gasconnading laughter
  and the panache of his heartbroken wit.

GEORGE V

Slowly the sceptre swings
     from right hand to left,
as the King of kings
     withdraws his gift.

Gently the crown and orb
     pass from his keeping,
where nothing can disturb,
     and there's no weeping.

The symbols of the throne
     seem a shadow only
for the soul that has grown,
     as all must, lonely.

But the dark that wrongs
     the king, must bow
to the man who belongs
     to the people now.

AS THE STARLIGHT EXCEEDS

As the starlight exceeds—he said.
  And as he spoke he burned
out and was dead.
  He had returned.

He threaded beauty; it is scattered
  like a string of beads.
But little that mattered
  " as the starlight exceeds ".

DEATH-MASK

So the sculptor carved her—
the pale Egyptian face
with the eyes hidden by the lashes.
None other deserved her,
since he alone could preserve her grace,
whose dark fingers dabble in the ashes.

RESURGET NUNQUAM

HERE Pierrot lies, his ruffles in the mud,
  outcast of love and honesty and law.
There eddies from his wounded side not blood
  but, as is proper with a puppet, straw.

EPITAPH

Now it is time to sleep.
I only ask
to be allowed to keep
unpierced the mask,
behind whose close
and changing covers
I hid myself from foes
        and lovers.